Narrative Discipleship

Narrative Discipleship

Portraits of Women in the Gospel of Mark

JEFFREY W. AERNIE

☙PICKWICK *Publications* · Eugene, Oregon

NARRATIVE DISCIPLESHIP
Portraits of Women in the Gospel of Mark

Copyright © 2018 Jeffrey W. Aernie. All rights reserved. Except for brief quotations in critical publications or reviews, no part of this book may be reproduced in any manner without prior written permission from the publisher. Write: Permissions, Wipf and Stock Publishers, 199 W. 8th Ave., Suite 3, Eugene, OR 97401.

Pickwick Publications
An Imprint of Wipf and Stock Publishers
199 W. 8th Ave., Suite 3
Eugene, OR 97401

www.wipfandstock.com

PAPERBACK ISBN: 978-1-5326-4421-4
HARDCOVER ISBN: 978-1-5326-4422-1
EBOOK ISBN: 978-1-5326-4423-8

Cataloging-in-Publication data:

Names: Aernie, Jeffrey W.

Title: Narrative discipleship : portraits of women in the Gospel of Mark / by Jeffrey W. Aernie.

Description: Eugene, OR : Pickwick Publications, 2018 | Includes bibliographical references and indexes.

Identifiers: ISBN 978-1-5326-4421-4 (paperback) | ISBN 978-1-5326-4422-1 (hardcover) | ISBN 978-1-5326-4423-8 (ebook)

Subjects: LCSH: Bible. Mark—Criticism, interpretation, etc. | Women in the Bible. | Christian life—Biblical teaching. | Bible. Mark—Criticism, Narrative.

Classification: LCC BS2585.52 A3 2018 (print) | LCC BS2585.52 (ebook)

Manufactured in the U.S.A.   07/19/18

For Abigail Jean, Chloe Anne, and Rebekah Grace,
may you learn to be faithful disciples of Christ

Contents

Acknowledgments | ix
Abbreviations | xi

Introduction | 1

Part One—**Narratives *and* Discipleship**
1 Narrative Exegesis | 9
2 Markan Discipleship | 28

Part Two—**Narratives *of* Discipleship**
3 Restored Discipleship (Mark 1 and 5) | 47
4 Spoken Discipleship (Mark 7) | 67
5 Active Discipleship (Mark 12 and 14) | 82
6 Cruciform Discipleship (Mark 15–16) | 101

Conclusion | 119

Bibliography | 125
Index of Authors | 133
Index of Ancient Sources | 137

Acknowledgments

My initial engagement with the narratives of the women in Mark's Gospel coincided with my appointment as Lecturer in New Testament Studies at Charles Sturt University (United Theological College) in Sydney, Australia. My former colleague, Jione Havea, invited me to contribute to a project that would examine the theological significance of borders in Scripture. My essay on the Syrophoenician woman for that volume fostered an ongoing fascination with the narrative contours of Mark's Gospel. In retrospect, although I was focused on the impact of geographical and theological borders in Mark 7, I was traversing a number of contextual borders in my own life—from postgraduate student to faculty member, from residence in the northern hemisphere to the southern hemisphere, and from a focus in my academic work on the Pauline epistles to the Synoptic Gospels. Each of these border crossings influenced the development of this book. I am grateful to the leadership at United Theological College for providing time and funding for research. I appreciate colleagues in Australia who have helped expand my cultural and exegetical purview. And I am indebted to those scholars whose work on the narratives of the women in Mark's Gospel has been invaluable in shaping my own thinking on the way in which this character group contributes to Mark's portrait of discipleship.

I want to express my appreciation to those colleagues and friends who carved out time from their own obligations and projects to offer constructive feedback and insightful criticism. Their wisdom sharpened my thinking at every stage. Special thanks are due to Matthew Aernie, Jonathan Hoffman, Dave Keun, Jason Maston, Benjamin Myers, David Neville, and Anthony Rees. I had the opportunity to trial sections of the book in a number of arenas, both academic and ecclesial. I appreciate the encouragement and engagement that I received in each of those contexts. Special thanks are due to Richard Harris (Terrigal Uniting Church) and John Court (Eastwood

Acknowledgments

Uniting Church) who graciously invited me to engage in extended conversations on the portrait of discipleship in Mark's Gospel.

I am enriched in my own pursuit of faithful discipleship by my wife, Allison. Her sacrificial love, persistent encouragement, and incisive questions were essential catalysts for the creation and completion of this project. In exploring the portraits of faithful women who embody the reality of God's kingdom I am keenly aware that Allison and I have been blessed with three daughters and charged with the responsibility for their spiritual formation. My prayer for them is that they too would grow to be women who embody the reality of God's kingdom in belief and action. I dedicate this book to them.

Two chapters of this book represent significantly revised versions of earlier publications. Chapter 4 is a revision of "Borderless Discipleship: The Syrophoenician Woman as a Christ-Follower in Mark 7:24–30," in *Bible, Borders, Belonging(s): Engaging Readers from Oceania*, edited by Jione Havea, David Neville, and Elaine Wainwright, 191–207, Semeia Studies 75 (Atlanta: Society of Biblical Literature, 2014). Chapter 6 is a revision of "Cruciform Discipleship: The Narrative Function of the Women in Mark 15–16," *JBL* 135 (2016) 779–797. I am grateful to the Society of Biblical Literature for permission to use both of these earlier pieces in their revised form.

Abbreviations

AB	Anchor Bible
ABRL	Anchor Bible Reference Library
ANRW	*Aufstieg und Niedergang der römischen Welt: Geschichte und Kultur Roms im Spiegel der neueren Forschung.* Part 2, Principat. Edited by Hildegard Temporini and Wolfgang Haase. Berlin: de Gruyter, 1972–
ANTC	Abingdon New Testament Commentaries
BAR	*Biblical Archeology Review*
BBR	*Bulletin for Biblical Research*
BDF	Blass, Friedrich, Albert Debrunner, and Robert W. Funk. *A Greek Grammar of the New Testament and Other Early Christian Literature.* Chicago: University of Chicago Press, 1961
BECNT	Baker Exegetical Commentary on the New Testament
Bib	*Biblica*
BibInt	*Biblical Interpretation*
BNTC	Black's New Testament Commentaries
BTB	*Biblical Theology Bulletin*
BTS	Biblical Tools and Studies
CBQ	*Catholic Biblical Quarterly*
CurTM	*Currents in Theology and Mission*
ExpTim	*Expository Times*
GBS	Guides to Biblical Scholarship

Abbreviations

Int	*Interpretation*
JAAR	*Journal for the American Academy of Religion*
JBL	*Journal of Biblical Literature*
JETS	*Journal of the Evangelical Theological Society*
JR	*Journal of Religion*
JSNT	*Journal for the Study of the New Testament*
JSNTsup	Journal for the Study of the New Testament Supplement Series
JTSA	*Journal of Theology for Southern Africa*
LNTS	Library of New Testament Studies
NIBCNT	New International Biblical Commentary on the New Testament
NICNT	New International Commentary on the New Testament
NIGTC	New International Greek Testament Commentary
NTL	New Testament Library
NTS	*New Testament Studies*
PRSt	*Perspectives in Religious Studies*
RBS	Resources for Biblical Study
RNT	Regensburger Neues Testament
RTR	*Reformed Theological Review*
SBFA	Studium Biblicum Franciscanum Analecta
SNTSMS	Society for New Testament Studies Manuscript Series
SNTW	Studies of the New Testament and Its World
SP	Sacra Pagina
SSEJC	Studies in Scripture in Early Judaism and Christianity
TNTC	Tyndale New Testament Commentaries
WBC	Word Biblical Commentary
WUNT	Wissenschaftliche Untersuchungen zum Neuen Testament
WW	*Word and World*

Introduction

NARRATIVE DISCIPLESHIP—A PROPOSAL

MARK'S GOSPEL IS A narrative proclamation of God's in-breaking kingdom that seeks to shape the lives of its audience. The progression of the Gospel from the prophetic proclamation of the good news concerning the messianic identity of Jesus to the culmination of this good news in the resurrection of the crucified Jesus compels us to recognize Jesus as the king of a renewed and restored creation. The intent of this dramatic narrative of God's kingdom breaking into the world in Jesus is to call us to participate in this new kingdom as those who faithfully embody its reality in belief and action. This enacted participation in God's kingdom is the definition of Markan discipleship. Within Mark's Gospel the narrative of Christ creates the narrative of those who follow him. The portrait of discipleship that Mark develops in his narrative of God's in-breaking kingdom is conditioned by the life, death, and resurrection of Jesus. Discipleship for Mark entails an active embodiment of the reality and implication of Christ's inauguration of a renewed creation and a reordered humanity.

Markan discipleship is rooted in the narrative of Jesus. There is an inseparable link in Mark's Gospel between Christology—what the narrative proclaims about the identity and mission of Jesus—and discipleship—what the narrative asserts about the identity and mission of those who desire to follow Jesus. A key way that Mark demonstrates this connection is through the intersection of the narrative of Jesus with the narratives of other characters. The distinct characters that feature in the Gospel elucidate Mark's definition of discipleship as they interact with and respond to Jesus. The

Introduction

twelve disciples are a constructive example of this process. Their extensive engagement with Jesus creates a unique portrait of the radical demands of Markan discipleship. The aim of this volume is to demonstrate how Mark's narrative portrayal of women extends the portrait of discipleship that he creates for his audience.

In his otherwise insightful volume *The Theology of the Gospel of Mark*, William Telford suggests that the women in Mark's Gospel "are essentially minor characters who do little in the context of the Gospel to propel the plot forward."[1] Telford's largely negative assessment of the women is built on the confined role that they have in comparison to the twelve disciples and other male characters. In spite of the limited narrative space that the women occupy as minor characters in Mark's Gospel, my contention is that Mark narrates specific stories of women as an essential dimension of the plot's development. Mark's intentional portrayal of eight women—Simon's mother-in-law (Mark 1:29–31), the bleeding woman (Mark 5:25–34), the Syrophoenician woman (Mark 7:24–30), the poor widow (Mark 12:41–44), the woman who anoints Jesus (Mark 14:3–9), and the three named women in the passion narrative (Mark 15:40–41, 47; 16:1–8)—contributes to the theological progression of the Gospel.[2] These women are exemplars of discipleship who serve as narrative representatives of the way in which God's in-breaking kingdom renews creation and reorders humanity.

My intention is to demonstrate how these eight women function together as a distinct character group within the Gospel narrative to extend Mark's theological portrait of discipleship. In specific terms, my aim is to describe how Mark's depiction of these women creates a portrait of *narrative discipleship*. To explain that we learn about the nature of Jesus's identity and mission only through our engagement with the narrated events of the Gospel, Robert Tannehill helpfully describes Mark's portrayal of Jesus as "narrative Christology."[3] The form of Mark's theological communication shapes the way we learn from it and respond to it. In the same way, as the

---

1. Telford, *Theology of the Gospel of Mark*, 232.

2. In addition to these eight women, Mark's narrative features Jesus's mother, Mary, and his sisters (Mark 3:20–35), Jairus's daughter (Mark 5:21–24; 35–43), Herodias and her daughter (Mark 6:14–29), the Syrophoenician woman's daughter (Mark 7:24–30), the parabolic widow of seven husbands (Mark 12:18–27), the servant woman who interrogates Peter (Mark 14:66–72), and the large group of unnamed women who followed Jesus from Galilee to Jerusalem (Mark 15:41). In addition to the material that follows on these women, see esp. Miller, *Women in Mark's Gospel*.

3. Tannehill, "Gospel of Mark as Narrative Christology," 57–95.

Introduction

audience of Mark's Gospel, we learn to define discipleship only through our engagement with its narrated events. Mark's portrayal of the women develops narrative discipleship just as his portrayal of Jesus develops narrative Christology. The goal of Mark's portrayal of these women is not to encourage his audience to imitate their specific actions. Our historical context means it is impossible to do this. We cannot touch Jesus's clothes from behind in the midst of the crowd (Mark 5:25–34) or anoint him with expensive perfume in preparation for his burial (Mark 14:3–9). In contrast, Mark's goal is to provide a narrative expression of what it means to embody characteristics that are essential to the nature and reality of God's in-breaking kingdom.

By using the phrase narrative discipleship my goal is to demonstrate that it is the thematic emphases of the women's individual narratives which extend the theological framework in which the life of discipleship can be worked out. As narrative representations of essential characteristics of Markan discipleship—restored life, kingdom speech, sacrificial action, and cruciformity—these women are a key bridge in the communicative act between author and audience. Mark integrates their individual stories into the wider narrative of God's in-breaking kingdom so that the audience of the Gospel—both ancient and contemporary—can learn to embody these characteristics of discipleship in its own context. That is, Mark seeks to convert the imagination of his audience—to reshape us both cognitively and affectively so that we can participate in the kingdom as faithful followers of Jesus.[4]

As an act of theological communication with intent the Gospel displays narrative discipleship to create real disciples. As David Neville so helpfully notes in his treatment of the ethical implications of Mark's Gospel, both the specific teachings of Jesus that Mark narrates and the entire narrative world created in the Gospel impacts the audience in such a way "so as to shape or reshape, challenge or reinforce attitudes and priorities."[5] Neville continues:

> Mark's narrative as a whole, but also any particular part within it, bristles with the potential to alter perspective, transform understanding, provoke character evaluation, and reorient assumptions about the nature of reality and standard patterns of human

---

4. For the language of "conversion of the imagination," see Hays, *Conversion of the Imagination*.

5. Neville, *Peaceable Hope*, 47.

Introduction

relationships, all of which are either profoundly moral in and of themselves or have moral implications. In this respect, the programmatic summary in Mark 1:14–15 is instructive. Jesus's proclamation of the good news *concerning God* . . . calls for radical reorientation that leads to the possibility of a life of faith and a faithful life.[6]

The individual narratives of the eight women examined in the present volume bristle with this "radical reorientation" as the themes embodied in their narratives elucidate Mark's description of the way in which God's kingdom breaks into the world in the life, death, and resurrection of Jesus. These women function as narrative representatives of the good news. As they embody and participate in the restoration, speech, action, and cruciformity of the kingdom, they are *narrative disciples* and they portray *narrative discipleship*.

For those captured by Mark's theological vision of God's in-breaking kingdom, the impetus of the Gospel is to imagine ways to reflect and participate in the kingdom-oriented characteristics portrayed in the individual narratives of these eight women. The goal is to move from *narrative discipleship* to *embodied discipleship*. This task requires more than simply trying to imitate the ways in which these women engage with Jesus. The women's narrative discipleship is not a strict paradigm meant to condition the specific actions of the audience. The women's narrative discipleship is a call to a reimagined form of discipleship that seeks to respond to the reality of God's kingdom and to demonstrate commitment to the crucified and resurrected Jesus.

NARRATIVE DISCIPLESHIP—A THESIS

My thesis in basic terms is that Mark narrates the stories of eight women in the Gospel to extend the portrait of discipleship that he creates for his audience. This thesis contains three key components. First, Mark intentionally crafts the material that we encounter in the narrative of the Gospel. Mark's Gospel is not a mere recitation of historical events or an uncreative compilation of source material. Mark shapes biographical, historical, and scriptural content into a coherent narrative about the reality of God's in-breaking kingdom in the life, death, and resurrection of Jesus. The portraits of the women are a component of this intentional composition. They are

6. Ibid., 48 (emphasis original).

Introduction

incorporated into the narrative of the Gospel to support its theological development.

Second, Mark intentionally crafts this narrative about God's in-breaking kingdom to foster discipleship. As an act of theological communication the Gospel intends to shape the life of its audience. In this way the Gospel is aretegenic—it seeks to create a particular form of embodied virtue.[7] Virtue in this context is not merely a form of mental assent or trust but a form of allegiance in which the audience of the Gospel is called to participate in the narrative of God's in-breaking kingdom.[8] This virtue or allegiance—this *discipleship*—is a dynamic activity which requires an active embodiment of the transformative reality of God's kingdom and a faithful allegiance to the crucified and resurrected Jesus.

Third, one of the key ways that Mark intentionally communicates this form of holistic discipleship is through the portrayal of eight women—Simon's mother-in-law (Mark 1:29–31), the bleeding woman (Mark 5:25–34), the Syrophoenician woman (Mark 7:24–30), the poor widow (Mark 12:41–44), the woman who anoints Jesus (Mark 14:3–9), and the three named women in the passion narrative (Mark 15:40–41, 47; 16:1–8). The narratives of these women are essential as they reflect the transformation and allegiance inherent in Mark's portrayal of discipleship. Although their narratives occur in isolated scenes throughout the Gospel, Mark's portrayal of these women functions as a cohesive narrative device. Their individual narratives create a composite reflection of four essential components of Markan discipleship—restored life, kingdom speech, sacrificial action, and cruciformity.

NARRATIVE DISCIPLESHIP—A STRUCTURE

To develop each of the components of this thesis the following material is divided into two parts. Part one consists of two chapters that provide the methodological and thematic framework for the extended exegetical examinations of the individual narratives of the women in Mark's Gospel that comprise part two. Chapter 1 engages the narrative dimensions of

---

7. For the introduction of the adjective aretegenic ("virtue-forming") in theological discourse, see Charry, *By the Renewing of Your Minds*, 16–19. Cf. Pennington, *Sermon on the Mount and Human Flourishing*, 15–16.

8. For the use of the language of allegiance to describe the narrative impact of the Gospels, see Bates, *Salvation by Allegiance Alone*.

Introduction

Mark's Gospel. My intention here is to offer an introduction to the interpretation of narrative texts with a specific focus on the study of characters. This will allow us to see how Mark develops the narratives of the women to form a composite character group within the Gospel. Chapter 2 examines the wider theme of discipleship and the portrait of the twelve disciples in Mark's Gospel. The portrait of discipleship that Mark creates through his characterization of these eight women does not constitute the entirety of his definition of discipleship. Rather, a key aspect of my thesis is that Mark's portrait of the women extends his definition of discipleship through the kingdom-oriented themes embedded in their narratives. The intention of this chapter, therefore, is to describe the wider framework of discipleship in Mark's Gospel to better understand how the women—as a distinct character group—contribute to its definition and development.

Part two consists of four chapters that interpret the individual narratives of eight women in the Gospel to determine how they contribute to our understanding of the wider theme of discipleship. Chapter 3 examines the portraits of two women—Simon's mother-in-law (Mark 1:29–31) and the bleeding woman (Mark 5:25–34). Each of these narratives highlights the theme of restored life. These women encounter Jesus and are transformed by the restorative power of God's kingdom. Chapter 4 focuses on the dramatic narrative of Jesus's interaction with the Syrophoenician woman (Mark 7:24–30). Her narrative portrays the necessity of kingdom speech. The woman's interaction with Jesus functions as an act of proclamation about the reality of God's in-breaking kingdom. Chapter 5 considers the portraits of two women—a poor widow (Mark 12:41–44) and the woman who anoints Jesus (Mark 14:3–9). The narratives of these two women are portraits of sacrificial action. Mark emphasizes the way in which each woman embodies the sacrificial reversal inherent in God's new kingdom. Chapter 6 reconsiders the extended portrait of the three named women in Mark's passion narrative (Mark 15:40–41, 47; 16:1–8). In contrast to the broad consensus that the narrative of these three women ends in failure, I will argue that they are narrative representations of cruciformity. Their direct association with the climactic events of Mark's narrative—Jesus's crucifixion, burial, and resurrection—positions them as exemplars of the cruciform commitment required by God's kingdom.

Part One—Narratives *and* Discipleship

1

Narrative Exegesis

INTRODUCTION

MARK'S GOSPEL IS A story. Although we sometimes read the Gospel in fragmented ways—examining the significance of individual miracle stories or considering the intention of specific parables—the Gospel itself is a holistic and unified narrative which portrays the way in which Jesus brings about the in-breaking of God's kingdom through his life, death, and resurrection.[1] Because Mark's Gospel is a narrative it is important that we read and interpret it as a narrative. Constructive interpretation of the Gospel requires what I want to refer to as *narrative exegesis*. The phrase "narrative exegesis" is intended to denote the basic idea that our interpretation of any narrative text needs to reckon with the literary nature of the text itself. Since Mark's Gospel is a narrative, our exegesis (or interpretation) of the Gospel needs to consider its various narrative components and characteristics (e.g., characters, plot, and setting). In the same way that effectively reading a newspaper editorial or a cookbook recipe requires an awareness of its genre, reading and interpreting Mark's Gospel requires a particular

1. The seminal work in defining Mark's Gospel as a narrative is Rhoads and Michie, *Mark as Story*. As a testimony to its impact, the volume was revised extensively in a second edition: Rhoads, Dewey, and Michie, *Mark as Story* (1999). It has now been published in a third edition: Rhoads, Dewey, and Michie, *Mark as Story* (2012). Unless otherwise noted, subsequent references are to the third edition. For a discussion of the influence of the book, see Iverson and Skinner, *Mark as Story*.

Part One—Narratives *and* Discipleship

orientation to the shape and nature of its narrative. The way in which we orient ourselves toward the Gospel impacts our evaluation of its meaning and our response to its theological agenda.

My intention within this chapter is to explain how the rest of the volume will orient itself toward Mark's Gospel. There are two components to this orientation: (1) a brief rationale for focusing on Mark's Gospel as a narrative, and (2) an explanation of the significance of Mark's portrayal of a specific set of characters within the Gospel—the women. These dual aims provide the basic framework for the material that follows. The first section of the chapter provides an introduction to narrative analysis of Mark's Gospel with a particular focus on defining the interpretive framework that will be used in the exegetical chapters in part two. The second section of the chapter then provides an introduction to the specific concept of characterization—the way in which Mark intentionally develops portraits of characters to support the development of the Gospel's theological agenda.

NARRATIVE CRITICISM AND THE GOSPEL OF MARK

Recognition of the need to interpret Mark's Gospel as a unified story normally takes place in biblical scholarship within the framework of narrative criticism. Narrative criticism is a method unique to the field of biblical studies which uses insights from the discipline of literary criticism (the critical study of literary texts) to explore scriptural narratives.[2] To define it in basic terms, narrative criticism is a method of interpretation that examines the literary characteristics of a narrative to determine how that narrative is intended to impact its audience. For example, we might inquire as to how the structured narrative of Mark's Gospel encourages its audience to consider and to respond to the identity of Jesus. To this end, narrative critics are predominantly interested in two key components of a narrative—its story and discourse. In this context, the term "story" refers to the content of the narrative and the term "discourse" refers to the shape of the narrative.[3] More specifically, the term "story" refers to the actual components of a narrative, such as the characters portrayed or the events described, and the term

---

2. The most accessible introduction to narrative criticism is Powell, *What Is Narrative Criticism*. See also Marguerat and Bourquin, *How to Read Bible Stories*; and Resseguie, *Narrative Criticism*. The phrase "narrative criticism" was first introduced in Rhoads, "Narrative Criticism," 411–26.

3. Malbon, "Narrative Criticism," 32; Powell, *What Is Narrative Criticism*, 23.

Narrative Exegesis

"discourse" refers to the way in which those elements are organized into a unified whole. The primary aim of narrative criticism is to understand how the intentional organization (discourse) of specific narrative elements (story) impacts the audience.[4]

Applied specifically to Mark's Gospel, the intent of narrative criticism is to examine the way in which the Gospel narrative interacts with and impacts upon its audience. In determining how the narrative elements of the story are structured within the discourse of the Gospel, we hope to gain insight into Mark's expectation for the way his audience will respond to his presentation of the narrative of Jesus's life, death, and resurrection. In other words, we are interested in examining how Mark's intentional organization of the plot, events, settings, and characters within the Gospel narrative impacts the audience's response to Jesus. In the present volume our focus is on the way in which Mark portrays a specific group of characters within the narrative—the women—as a means to develop a portrait of discipleship that the audience may either accept or reject depending upon how they respond—both cognitively and affectively—to the shape of Mark's narrative. We want to know how Mark's narrative portrayal of the women functions as part of the aretegenic purpose of the Gospel to explain the good news about Jesus (Mark 1:1). This form of examination is built on three components: (1) engagement with the Gospel as a cohesive narrative, (2) narrative exegesis of individual narratives, and (3) analysis of the aretegenic (virtue-forming) nature of the narrative.[5]

The Gospel of Mark as a Cohesive Narrative

James Resseguie helpfully notes that "Narrative critics are interested in narratives as complete tapestries in which the parts fit together to form an organic whole."[6] For the most part narrative criticism is not concerned with explaining the historical process behind the creation of a text (e.g., who was Mark and what sources did he have available to him?) but rather

---

4. Cf. Powell, "Narrative Criticism: The Emergence of a Prominent Reading Strategy," 23.

5. These components are constructed from what Resseguie refers to as the three areas of "usefulness of narrative criticism." He argues that narrative criticism: (1) "views the text as a whole," (2) "examines the complexities and nuances of a text through close readings," and (3) "emphasizes the effects of a narrative on the reader" (*Narrative Criticism*, 38–40).

6. Resseguie, *Narrative Criticism*, 39.

Part One—Narratives *and* Discipleship

with determining how a text behaves and communicates as a complete narrative. The focus of narrative criticism is not on the historical *construction* of a narrative, but on how the narrative *as constructed* functions as a meaningful piece of communication.[7] If we approach the Gospel merely as a compilation of distinct fragments, then it is difficult to argue for any form of intentional point of view within the material. In contrast, if we approach the Gospel as an intentionally and creatively crafted piece of communication, then we are able to examine its story, discourse, and impact.[8]

Within biblical studies the genesis of narrative criticism came about in large measure because of an emerging dissatisfaction with several other critical methods of interpretation—such as source, form, and redaction criticism—because of their relative inability to interact with the Gospels as cohesive narratives.[9] Although these methods provide insight into the historical construction and development of the Gospels, they tend not to examine the holistic nature of the Gospel narratives themselves. Source criticism, for example, provides valuable insight into the literary interdependence of the Gospels, but it does not provide an analysis of the Gospels as integrated narratives in their own right. Similarly, redaction criticism constructively identifies the writers of the Gospels as intentional authors as opposed to mere compilers, but it often creates an unhelpful distinction between original source material ("the tradition") and edited content ("the redaction"). The use of narrative criticism within biblical studies seeks to redress these deficiencies by paying special attention to the cohesive nature of the Gospel narratives. As narrative criticism has been applied specifically to Mark's Gospel a general consensus has emerged which views the Gospel as an integrated narrative with a clear rhetorical impact in relation to its audience.[10] Approaching Mark's Gospel as a unified narrative with

---

7. On the importance of the language of communication in narrative criticism, see esp. Sternberg, *The Poetics of Biblical Narrative*.

8. This is not to say that it is essential that Mark's narrative be uniform in every respect. Narratives—whether the Gospel or any another piece of literature—may create ambiguity, tension, or polyvalence. Rather, the argument is that Mark's narrative is *cohesive*. Without identifying a text as a cohesive narrative it would be impossible to discern whether challenging or polyvalent material represented an intentional dimension of the narrative discourse or was merely the unintended by-product of the compilation of distinct source material.

9. Powell, *What Is Narrative Criticism*, 1–10.

10. See, esp., Rhoads, Dewey, and Michie, *Mark as Story*, 3–4.

Narrative Exegesis

a particular theological point of view will be crucial for our subsequent analysis of the narratives of women within the Gospel.

None of this focus on the cohesive nature of the Gospel, however, is meant to suggest that narrative criticism is disinterested in either history or historical context. In contrast, the historical context of a narrative is a crucial dimension in our evaluation of its impact on its audience—both ancient and contemporary. The distinction between historical-critical study (e.g., source, form, and redaction criticism) and literary-critical study (e.g., narrative criticism) is best defined not in terms of incompatibility, but rather as a distinction with respect to reference or orientation. As Mark Alan Powell notes:

> Granted that the Gospels may function referentially as records of significant history, might they not also function poetically as stories that fire the imagination, provoke repentance, inspire worship, and so on? Or to put it another way, historical criticism may be said to treat biblical narratives as windows that enable us to learn something about another time and place; narrative criticism treats these same texts as mirrors that invite audience participation in the creation of meaning.[11]

It may be helpful to blur the line of this distinction even further. Cornelis Bennema suggests that a constructive step forward would be to develop "a form of *historical narrative criticism* that takes a text-centered approach but examines aspects of the world outside or 'behind' the text if the text invites us to do so."[12] Because the Gospels are narratives rooted in history, our literary analysis can be informed by the historical material which is embedded in the narrative itself. In light of this intersection between narrative and history, the subsequent exegetical material will aim to be cognizant both of the Gospel's status as a self-contained narrative with a particular theological trajectory and the reality that it is a narrative embedded within a particular historical context that may at times shape both the presentation of the story and the story itself. This dual focus will be central to the form of interpretation that I refer to as narrative exegesis.

---

11. Powell, "Narrative Criticism," 240.
12. Bennema, *Theory of Character*, 67 (emphasis original).

Part One—Narratives *and* Discipleship

Exegesis of the Narrative

Engaging in this form of historical narrative criticism means developing a constructive balance in our exegetical method between an analysis of the world of the text and that of the world behind the text. Because the main focus in the present volume is on a specific component of Mark's narrative, my primary emphasis is on the dynamics of the way in which specific narrative elements (story) are integrated into the narrative of the Gospel (discourse).[13] The historical context of Mark's narrative will be essential for understanding both elements of story and discourse, but my starting point is the final (canonical) form of the Gospel (Mark 1:1—16:8).[14] The examination of the specific portraits of women in the Gospel will concentrate on the way Mark integrates their individual narratives into his broader thematic presentation of discipleship. Mark's intentional organization and composition of the Gospel suggest that the narratives of these women are essential with respect to the development of the Gospel narrative itself. While elements of the historical context of the Gospel—such as the cultural identity of the Syrophoenician woman (Mark 7:24-30) and the economic position of the poor widow (Mark 12:41-44)—impact the shape of each woman's narrative, the position and function of these individual stories within the wider narrative and their connection with the theme of discipleship is the central focus in what follows.

A holistic reading of Mark's Gospel within the framework of narrative criticism would require a commentary length assessment of the entire narrative.[15] This stems from the reality that narrative criticism as a methodology provides space to examine an extensive amount of concepts in relation to the Gospel as narrative. These include, for example, assessments of the interaction between the implied author, narrator, and implied audience, examination of the plot, character, and setting, and evaluation of concepts

---

13. Cf. Powell, "Toward a Narrative-Critical Understanding," 341–46.

14. For a survey of the way in which scholars have understood the ending of Mark's Gospel, see Driggers, *Following God through Mark*, 86–96; and Williams, "Literary Approaches," 21–35. I assume that Mark 16:8 represents the intentional ending of the Gospel. For a survey of the text-critical issues, see Metzger, *Textual Commentary*, 102–6; and Stein, "Ending of Mark," 79–98. For a substantive argument in support of Mark 16:9–20 as the original ending, see Lunn, *Original Ending of Mark*.

15. For a narrative-critical commentary on Mark's Gospel, see Moloney, *Gospel of Mark*.

Narrative Exegesis

such as point of view and rhetoric.[16] All of these are important areas of study within narrative criticism. The goal of the present volume, however, is to trace the way in which Mark's portrayal of women in the narrative is intended to impact the audience's conception and reception of the theme of discipleship. The purpose, therefore, is not to examine all of the aspects of interpretation potentially developed under the umbrella of narrative criticism. In contrast, my goal is to exegete particular sections of Mark's Gospel to examine their connection with Mark's presentation of discipleship and how they might impact the audience's response to the narrative. This is what I mean by the phrase *narrative exegesis*: analyzing specific passages in the Gospel to ascertain their thematic and theological contribution to the wider narrative.

The chapters in part two will pay primary attention to the major components of the narrative's story (e.g., character, setting, and plot) and the shape of the narrative's discourse.[17] Again, the specific area I want to explore is how Mark's portrayal of certain women in the progression of the Gospel narrative extends his presentation of the theme of discipleship. Or, to phrase it as a question, how does Mark seek to impact the audience's response to Jesus through the portrayal of these women? What I hope to demonstrate is that certain aspects of discipleship are emphasized in the individual narratives of these women to create a composite portrait of discipleship meant to encourage the audience to participate in the reality of God's kingdom as faithful followers of Jesus. One of Mark's intentions in developing these specific narratives is to encourage the audience to align itself with the theological viewpoint of the Gospel—to follow Jesus and to embody the message of good news about him.

The Gospel of Mark as an Aretegenic Narrative

The interpretation of Mark's Gospel as a narrative allows us to engage with it as a piece of meaningful communication intended to impact its audience. Communication is not a static process contingent solely on the transfer of information from one source to another. Communication is a dynamic process that involves mutual engagement. With respect to Mark's Gospel, the text is an instance of communication between author and audience.[18]

16. Rhoads, Dewey, and Michie, *Mark as Story*.
17. Cf. Wegener, *Cruciformed*, 9–10.
18. Narrative criticism develops a more nuanced portrait of the process of

Part One—Narratives *and* Discipleship

Studying the narrative dimensions of the Gospel provides us with an opportunity to enter into that act of communication as a contemporary audience of the narrative. If we work with the notion that the author has crafted the narrative to elicit a specific set of responses from the audience, then the process of narrative exegesis helps us to define more clearly the response which the author hopes the audience will embody. By identifying the point of view—or theological agenda—of the narrative we can then begin to traverse the hermeneutical gap between the narrative world of the text and our own contemporary context.[19] As we glean information about Mark's definition of the characteristics of discipleship in his portrayal of the women, then we can begin to define how the narrative of the Gospel intends for its implied audience to respond and we can begin to foster our own response. Identifying the portrait of discipleship developed within the narrative provides insight into the narrative itself and shapes our engagement with it.

This transition from the world of the narrative to a contemporary application of its impact is rooted in the nature of the Gospel itself. Again, as an instance of communication, Mark's Gospel is a dynamic entity intended to create a response. In the same way that a poem or a documentary seeks to elicit an emotional or pragmatic response in its audience, Mark's Gospel, as a narrative, has a rhetorical impact upon its audience. "For the narrative critic, texts shape the way readers understand themselves and their

---

communication that describes the distinction between the historical world behind the text and the narrative world of the text. This more nuanced portrait is frequently diagrammed as follows:

Historical Author → |Implied Author → Narrator → Narratee → Implied Audience| →Historical Audience
Narrative or Text

The benefit of this diagram is its focus on the integrated nature of the narrative with the implied author and implied audience as constructs within the narrative. For the sake of simplicity, I will use the term "Mark" or "author" to refer to the implied author of the narrative—the author we can construct from the narrative itself—and the term "audience" to refer to the implied audience of the narrative—the audience that we can construct from the narrative that is expected by the implied author to engage with and respond to the narrative. For the use of this diagram within the narrative-critical study of Mark's Gospel, see Malbon, "Narrative Criticism," 33. For its original introduction in literary criticism, see Chatman, *Story and Discourse*, 151.

19. I am, therefore, advocating a form of narrative analysis that Powell refers to as "text-oriented narrative criticism." See Powell, "Narrative Criticism: The Emergence of a Prominent Reading Strategy," 33–36.

Narrative Exegesis

own present circumstances."[20] Defining the type of impact the Gospel has, however, is essential for the shape of our analysis. To this end, Jonathan Pennington offers a constructive framework for understanding the Gospels. He defines the Gospels in the following way: "Our canonical Gospels are the *theological, historical, and aretological (virtue-forming) biographical narratives that retell the story and proclaim the significance of Jesus Christ, who through the power of the Spirit is the Restorer of God's reign.*"[21] Within the present context, I am particularly interested in Pennington's assertion that the Gospels are aretological or aretegenic (virtue-forming) narratives.

The notion that the Gospels are aretegenic allows us to explain the way in which Mark's Gospel impacts its audience. Identifying Mark's Gospel as a text that creates virtue encourages our involvement in responding to the narrative discourse. The Gospel not only provides theological and historical information, it incorporates those elements into a narrative—a text meant to be responded to by its audience. The specific response that Mark's Gospel develops is the theological formation of virtue. Or, to put it in the language of the present volume, the theological formation of discipleship. The outcome of our exegetical interpretation of Mark's Gospel is not merely the acquisition of information but an embodiment of the characteristics of discipleship developed there.[22] While historical, social, cultural, and contextual distinctions between the first century CE and the present will always create distinctions in the way the Gospel narrative impacts different audiences, its ability to create an embodied virtue—discipleship—transcends that contextual and temporal divide. Mark's intentional theological construction of the Gospel will always result in an impact on its audience—whether positive (acceptance of the theological viewpoint of the narrative) or negative (rejection of the theological viewpoint of the narrative). Mark's Gospel is not merely a narrative that was formed in history, it is a narrative that forms its audience throughout history.

---

20. Powell, "Narrative Criticism," 240.

21. Pennington, *Reading the Gospels Wisely*, 35 (emphasis original). For an extended introduction to the question of the genre of Mark's Gospel, see Collins, *Mark*, 15–43.

22. Cf. Rhoads, Dewey, and Michie, *Mark as Story*, 142: Mark's "narrative seeks to create ideal hearers who will establish solidarity with others who share the same values and commitments, in order to shape relationships and communities of mutual serving marked by faithfulness to the rule of God."

Part One—Narratives *and* Discipleship

CHARACTERIZATION AND THE GOSPEL OF MARK

One of the key ways that Mark's Gospel develops the theological narrative of God's re-creation and restoration of the world in Jesus is through the portrayal of characters. Examination of the function and impact of characters is a crucial component of narrative criticism. Within every narrative there is a strong connection between the progression of the plot and the portrayal of characters. The development of plot and character drives the narrative forward and provides the narrative space in which meaning and impact are constructed. Our analysis of Mark's Gospel is interested in the way a specific cross-section of characters—the women—contributes to the wider development of the plot and the construction of the theme of discipleship. To build an argument for the contribution of these individual narratives it is necessary for us to have a foundational understanding of the way in which Mark employs characters in the narrative. This foundational understanding involves three components: (1) a survey of the study of characters and characterization within narrative criticism, (2) a discussion of characters and characterization in Mark's Gospel, and (3) a rationale for analyzing the narratives of individual women in concert.

Characters and Characterization in Narrative Criticism

Characterization is the process by which an author develops the portrait of a character in a narrative. To employ the language of narrative criticism, characters exist at the level of story (the components of a narrative), whereas characterization exists at the level of discourse (the intentional organization of the narrative). Characterization describes how an author organizes, shapes, or employs characters within the narrative. Authors can present characters to their audience in distinct ways. One of the most basic constructs for understanding characterization is the classic early education activity in America called "show and tell" or what, in my Australian context, is often referred to as "news." In this activity children bring an object such as a cherished toy or stuffed animal to school to present it to their peers as an exercise in communication. As the American name highlights, the student must both *show* the object—to allow the other students to observe it—and *tell* about the object—perhaps describing its origin, significance, or purpose. Both aspects of the activity are intended to introduce the object in an informative way. Characterization is a similar process. Authors may "show"

Narrative Exegesis

characters by introducing them into the narrative and allowing them to behave or act in specific ways or they may "tell" characters by providing specific information to the audience about their identity or traits.[23] In using these strategies authors create distinct types of characters that advance the narrative both with regard to plot and purpose.

Characters are deployed to support the rhetorical agenda of the narrative. That is, the author of the narrative develops the identity and portrait of a character to achieve a particular goal.[24] As Elizabeth Struthers Malbon notes, "all the characters internal to the narrative exist not for their own sakes but for the sake of the communication between author and audience."[25] The portrait and role of a character are always conditioned by the overall intention (discourse) of the narrative. Even if characters represent specific historical figures (e.g., Simon's mother-in-law or Mary Magdalene), their portrayal in the narrative is conditioned by the shape of the narrative itself. Bennema's concise definition of character is useful here: "the term *character* refers to 'a human actor, individual or collective, imaginary or real, who plays a role in the story of a literary narrative.' While characters may resemble people, they only exist within the story world of the text (even when they represent real people in the real world)."[26] Bennema's definition is not meant to suggest that characters in a narrative are automatically unhistorical or fictitious. In contrast, it is a reminder that although the interpretation of narrative requires constructive knowledge of its historical context, narrative exegesis begins by examining the portrayal and function of characters within the final form of the narrative itself. With reference to the Gospels, the fact that they are theological texts rooted in history impacts the way in which we understand, reconstruct, and learn from the characters. But we understand, reconstruct, and learn from them within the boundaries established by Mark's narrative presentation. The impact that they have as characters exists within and stems from the narrative world of the Gospel.

The classification of characters that has been most influential within narrative criticism was developed at the beginning of the twentieth century by the literary critic E. M. Forster. Forster's basic typology described

---

23. Resseguie, *Narrative Criticism*, 126–30; Rhoads, Dewey, and Michie, *Mark as Story*, 100.
24. Cf. Burer, "Narrative Genre," 200.
25. Malbon, "Minor Characters," 61.
26. Bennema, *Theory of Character*, 29.

Part One—Narratives *and* Discipleship

characters as either "round" or "flat" depending on the level of complexity of the portrait of each character or character group in the narrative.[27] Round characters were those whose portrayal was more developed or complex. Flat characters were those whose portrayal was less developed or complex. To take Mark's Gospel as an example, the twelve disciples are defined as round characters because of the extensive and multifaceted nature of their portrayal. Simon's mother-in-law (Mark 1:29–31) and the poor widow (Mark 12:41–44) are defined as flat characters in light of their limited descriptions and roles. Their individual portraits do not reflect the complexity of Mark's characterization of the twelve disciples either in terms of the frequency of their presence ("show") or their narrative description ("tell").

Forster's basic typology is a constructive starting point for the study of character and characterization. It is important, however, to avoid the perception that all characters are either uniformly round or flat. Characters are not static entities defined in one of two ways but rather dynamic entities that can be portrayed along a spectrum of relationship.[28] An important example of this nuance is the paradigm of characterization developed by Bennema, who argues that we can classify characters in New Testament narratives along an aggregated continuum that takes account of factors including the complexity of their narrative portraits (the amount of traits a character exhibits in the narrative), the progression of their identities (how a character adapts or changes in the narrative), and the portrayal of their inner lives (information about a character's internal thoughts, emotions, or motivations).[29] Using this broader form of classification allows us to nuance our description of characters and to avoid the potential for reductionistic interpretations implicit in static readings of the flat–round model. It is also a reminder that characters—whether they are presented with simplicity or complexity—are dynamic entities which the author employs to enhance

27. Forster, *Aspects of the Novel*, esp. 103–25.

28. So Malbon, "Minor Characters," 82n6: "The main significance of the flat–round distinction is not that it allows us to label some characters flat (and possibly dismiss them) and others round (and possibly emphasize them) but that it forces us to consider each character in relation to all other characters. Flat and round are relative—and thus relational—terms."

29. Bennema, *Theory of Character*, 72–82. Bennema adapts these categories for biblical studies primarily in conversation with the work of Yosef Ewen. See Ewen, *Character in Narrative*, and Ewen, "Theory of Character," 1–30. For the crucial notion in biblical studies that characters can be plotted along a continuum, see esp. Burnett, "Characterization and Reader Construction," 3–28.

Narrative Exegesis

and progress the rhetorical agenda of the narrative. Characters function both to move the plot forward and to encourage the audience to respond to the plot.

Characters and Characterization in the Gospel of Mark

The characters in Mark's Gospel are essential to the development of Mark's theological agenda. As we consider the portrayal of characters and the process of characterization in Mark's Gospel, the insightful work of Bennema will be our primary guide. After an extensive survey of approaches to characters within both wider literary critical and narrative critical studies, Bennema develops an original paradigm for the analysis of characters in the New Testament. His paradigm consists of three components: (1) an analysis of characters with respect to text and context, (2) a classification of characters along a spectrum of complexity (introduced above), and (3) an evaluation of characters' relationship to the author's point of view and the narrative plot which helps to determine their contemporary significance.[30] Each of these three components offers constructive insights for our exegesis of the narratives of the individual women in Mark's Gospel. For this reason what follows is a more detailed description of Bennema's paradigm.

Bennema's first component—an analysis of characters with respect to text and context—has a dual focus. First, Bennema demonstrates the way in which our study of character and characterization needs to be conditioned by the type of narrative under investigation. Given the fact that Mark's Gospel is rooted in history, our "knowledge of the social and cultural environment of the New Testament is essential for understanding the personality, motive, and behavior of ancient characters."[31] Similarly, in his own study of a specific cross-section of characters in Mark's Gospel—the Gentiles—Kelly Iverson notes that the "social, historical, and cultural context of the first-century Mediterranean world is important for understanding the narrative of Mark's Gospel."[32] Along with Iverson, our focus in the present volume centers on the narrative world constructed within Mark's Gospel, but we too do not regard Mark's Gospel "as an autonomous story world that can be known in isolation from its socio-cultural context."[33] The

30. See Bennema, *Theory of Character*, 61–106.
31. Ibid., 62.
32. Iverson, *Gentiles in the Gospel of Mark*, 4.
33. Ibid., 4; cf. Malbon, "Jewish Leaders," 259–81: "a literary approach to Mark—as a

Part One—Narratives *and* Discipleship

historical context of Mark's Gospel impacts the way in which characters are constructed within the world of the narrative.

Bennema's second focus in the first component of his paradigm examines the identity of the audience. Understanding how a character will be perceived requires insight into the assumed knowledge of the audience. In line with his proposed form of historical narrative criticism, Bennema suggests that the most constructive approach is to consider an audience that is both historically informed and modern.[34] By "historically informed" Bennema means that the audience can realistically be assumed to possess knowledge of the world of the first century CE. Further, while an audience's knowledge of a particular character develops in the first instance from the world of the narrative it can also be shaped by other sources reasonably available. With respect to Mark's Gospel, for example, a historically informed reader would both know "the Old Testament and [have] informed knowledge of the first-century Jewish and Greco-Roman world."[35]

Bennema's second descriptor—"modern"—refers to the idea that our position as a contemporary audience without direct access to the first century CE requires a fusion of ancient and contemporary horizons. As those studying Mark's Gospel in a contemporary setting we insert ourselves into the narrative as the implied audience. In other words, as a contemporary audience we necessarily create the implied audience of the Gospel in our own image. We determine the boundaries of historical knowledge and our context will inevitably impact the way we interpret the narrative. As with our discussion of narrative criticism above, this form of reading is anticipated by and stems from the Gospel itself. As a narrative, Mark's Gospel is always intended to impact its audience. As a specifically aretegenic narrative it seeks not only to provide its audience with information, but to shape the way its audience lives (discipleship). Our interpretation of characters within the Gospel is an extension of this reality. The intentional portrayal of characters impacts our response to and engagement with the narrative.

Bennema's second component—the classification of characters along a spectrum of complexity—entails the creation of a system that maps characters along a continuum based on the way they are characterized (from

---

first-century work—is bounded by our understanding of its probable historical context" (274).

34. Bennema, *Theory of Character*, 68–71; cf. Powell, "Narrative Criticism: The Emergence of a Prominent Reading Strategy," 24.

35. Bennema, *Theory of Character*, 69.

Narrative Exegesis

agent to individual). As we noted above, Bennema adopts a classification system that examines three dimensions of the portrayal of characters: the complexity of their narrative portraits (the amount of traits a character exhibits in the narrative), the progression of their identities (how a character adapts or changes in the narrative), and the portrayal of their inner lives (information about a character's internal thoughts, emotions, or motivations).[36] There are two significant benefits to this classification system. First, by mapping characters along a continuum we can describe the process of characterization with more specificity. For example, within narrative analyses of Mark's Gospel Simon's mother-in-law (Mark 1:29–31) is often understood merely as a flat character with little narrative development. Bennema's classification system, however, allows us to examine the specific trait which she demonstrates—service—and how that trait develops in importance throughout the narrative. Second, this system provides a means of discussing the relationship between characters. The service of Simon's mother-in-law, for example, is important not only for her portrait as an individual character, but also for the way in which it defines her relationship with others who embody the trait of service, especially Jesus (Mark 10:45) and the women who follow Jesus from Galilee to Jerusalem (Mark 15:40–41).[37]

Bennema's third component—the evaluation of characters' relationship to the author's point of view and the narrative plot—examines characters with respect to the author's intended purpose.[38] The point of this component of Bennema's paradigm is that our narrative exegesis of Mark's Gospel needs not only to describe characters but also to evaluate them. Bennema's discussion of the concept of point of view is especially important.[39] Since Mark's Gospel is an intentionally crafted narrative that seeks to shape the life of its audience through its portrait of Jesus, it has a particular viewpoint (or theological agenda) within which individual characters can be evaluated. The way in which a character engages directly with Jesus or with the wider ethos of Mark's presentation impacts the way that the audience will respond to them, whether positively or negatively. As Bennema notes, "Mark's narrative reflects a worldview that is characterized by a

36. Ibid., 72–82.
37. Cf. ibid., 74–75. We will discuss the role of service in the narrative of Simon's mother-in-law more fully in ch. 3.
38. Ibid., 90–103.
39. Ibid., 90–91; cf. Rhoads, Dewey, and Michie, *Mark as Story*, 44–46.

Part One—Narratives *and* Discipleship

moral dualism—living on God's terms versus living on human terms—and characters embody one or the other."[40] The way in which we evaluate the women's connection to Mark's wider theological agenda will impact the way in which we apply the significance of their narratives in our own context.

The Women as Corporate Character in the Gospel of Mark

A key framework for the analysis of specific characters in Mark's Gospel has been the distinction between "major" and "minor" characters. Somewhat similar to Forster's flat-round classification of character types, the major-minor classification describes the portrayal of characters in terms of their narrative presence. Major characters—whether simple or complex—have a sustained or recurring presence in the narrative. Minor characters—whether simple or complex—lack a sustained or recurring presence in the narrative.[41] The usefulness of this classification is that it allows us to think more intentionally about the function of particular characters in relationship to others. That is, it provides us with another spectrum on which to plot the characters in the Gospel so that we can see how they compare and contrast with each other. In terms of our specific focus on the theme of discipleship, Mark can use minor characters, such as the women, to exemplify aspects of discipleship that may be misappropriated or neglected in his portrayal of the twelve disciples. To return to the work of Bennema, the "minor characters . . . significantly advance the plot of Mark's narrative because they function as primary examples of faith and discipleship."[42]

An essential contribution to our understanding of the minor characters in Mark's Gospel is the extensive analysis of character and characterization by Joel Williams.[43] Williams examines each of the minor characters in Mark's Gospel to demonstrate their narrative function and to explain Mark's intention for including them in the narrative at specific points. Of particular importance is Williams's discussion of the concept of narrative analogy for understanding the minor characters in Mark's Gospel.[44] Narrative analogy is a literary device in which an author invests individual scenes with similar story components (e.g., characters, plot, or settings)

40. Bennema, *Theory of Character*, 100.
41. Malbon, "Minor Characters," 60.
42. Bennema, *Theory of Character*, 102.
43. Williams, *Other Followers*.
44. Ibid., 36–54.

Narrative Exegesis

so that the audience is encouraged to identify connections between them and to evaluate the impact of their similarities and differences. One of the key outcomes of Williams's use of narrative analogy is the idea that the minor characters can be examined both with respect to their individual narratives and with respect to one another.[45] The minor characters relate not only to the other characters within their particular scenes (e.g., the bleeding woman and Jesus), they also form a corporate character within the narrative as their individual scenes communicate to the audience through their analogous content. In the words of Malbon, the "richness of Markan characterization is the interplay, comparisons, and contrasts between these characters and in their reaching out to the hearers/readers, both ancient and contemporary."[46] Even though these minor characters have limited narrative space in the Gospel, their connection with one another extends their narrative impact.

Although discussions of characterization normally center on the portrayal of a single individual or a single group, the concept of narrative analogy suggests that it is fruitful to emphasize the narrative connection between individuals who appear at different stages within the narrated story. The intent of the present volume is to build on Williams's use of the concept of narrative analogy in considering the development of Mark's portrait of discipleship. While Williams's intent was to offer an overall analysis of the minor characters in the Gospel, the present study is more narrowly focused on how the individual portraits of eight women form a cohesive component of Mark's portrait of discipleship despite their presence at separate points of the narrative. Although each of the women that we will examine in part two of the book may be understood as "flat" characters or "single trait" characters, when we view them *together* they become more complex and impactful characters within the narrative of the Gospel.

Mark's characterization of these women occurs on at least two planes. First, the story of each woman develops fully within its own narrative context. Simon's mother-in-law and the anonymous woman who anoints Jesus both have specific roles to play at the distinct stages of the narrative in which they are introduced. Second, however, Mark's characterization of each of these women also develops in conjunction with the others. As we progress through the narrative we can identify a pattern in which Mark portrays these predominantly anonymous women as embodying specific

45. Cf. Smith, *Lion with Wings*, 80.
46. Malbon, *In the Company of Jesus*, x.

Part One—Narratives *and* Discipleship

characteristics of discipleship that are essential to his wider narrative of God's in-breaking kingdom. The named women in Mark 15–16 then serve as a culmination of this literary pattern. They are the faithful disciples who witness Jesus's death, burial, and resurrection and become the first bearers of the good news that constitutes the heart of Mark's Gospel.[47] As a collective these women represent a complex corporate character that embodies a number of the traits which Mark presents as uniquely associated with Jesus's own ministry—restoration, speech, action, and cruciformity.

In the conclusion to his constructive study on the analysis of characters in the New Testament, Bennema identifies what he sees as a key area of further research on characterization in the Gospels, the aretegenic function of characterization:

> that is, the concept of characters as moral agents of transformation. We noted that the author communicates his particular perspective or point of view through the characters in the story, implicitly leading the reader to evaluate the characters, thus creating various degrees of affinity or distance with these characters. Additionally, the reader's evaluation of the characters also leads to the reader's self-evaluation. This implies that the characters are potential change agents—they have the ability to effect transformation in the reader. An examination of characters as moral agents in an ethical reading of the biblical narratives will enhance the discipline of virtue ethics.[48]

This book is an attempt to engage in this form of character evaluation. My interest—building on the language of both Pennington and Bennema—is to examine the aretegenic impact of the connected narratives of these individual women. The intent of the examination is to describe how Mark utilizes their narratives to create a paradigm of discipleship and to transform his audience. The exegetical chapters in part two, therefore, are meant to engage both with the narrative itself and with the narrative's transformative implications.

The corporate character in Mark's Gospel comprised of eight women—Simon's mother-in-law (Mark 1:29–31), the bleeding woman (Mark 5:25–34), the Syrophoenician woman (Mark 7:24–30), the poor widow (Mark 12:41–44), the woman who anoints Jesus (Mark 14:3–9), and the three named women in the passion narrative (Mark 15:40–41, 47;

---

47. For this positive reading of the women in Mark 15–16, see ch. 6.
48. Bennema, *Theory of Character*, 188–89.

16:1–8)—is an exemplar of what it means to live on God's terms. As we will see in part two, these eight women embody essential characteristics of discipleship that Mark develops within his narrative about the life, death, and resurrection of Jesus. In this way, these specific characters become integral to the wider movement of the narrative. Their embodiment of essential characteristics of discipleship marks the progression of the narrative itself.[49] And as a contemporary audience of their narratives we have an opportunity to embody the same characteristics of discipleship to which their narratives point.

CONCLUSION

The purpose of this chapter was to define an interpretive orientation to Mark's Gospel. I began by providing a description and rationale for the narrative lens that will shape the subsequent exegetical material. Specifically, I argued that Mark's Gospel is an intentionally crafted theological narrative which seeks to encourage its audience to embody the portrait of discipleship that it develops. Further, using the character theory of Bennema as a guide, I explored the notion that the Gospel enacts this agenda through the creation and presentation of characters. Characters within the Gospel provide a point at which the audience may begin to respond to the narrative, learning the intention of the Gospel through the way in which characters engage either directly with Jesus or with the wider ethos of Mark's narrative. While Bennema constructs his theory to create a consistent model by which to examine and compare characters,[50] my intention in the following material is to highlight Mark's overall characterization of the women in the Gospel. The exegetical chapters in part two, therefore, attempt to build on Bennema's paradigm by offering a narrative presentation of eight women in the Gospel, focusing on their position in the text, the nature of their portraits, and their connection to the theological viewpoint of the Gospel to evaluate their significance for a life of embodied discipleship.

---

49. Cf. ibid., 102, 102n104.
50. See ibid., 113–83, for Bennema's own application of his paradigm.

2

Markan Discipleship

INTRODUCTION

MARK'S GOSPEL IS A theological and aretegenic narrative. Mark constructs a creative description of the reality of God's in-breaking kingdom in the life, death, and resurrection of Jesus to compel his audience toward an embodiment of the kingdom. The Gospel moves toward virtue—toward *discipleship*. This movement develops not through a systematic description of the characteristics and qualifications of discipleship but rather through the progression of the narrative itself. One of the key ways that this narrative progression takes place is through the intentional portrayal of characters. Characters are for the audience a point at which to enter the world of the narrative and to shape an imaginative response. Perhaps unsurprisingly, an important part of Mark's portrait of discipleship stems from the relational intersection between Jesus and the twelve disciples. The extensive narrative presence of the twelve disciples provides a framework for the definition and demands of discipleship. It is within this framework that we can begin to understand the unique contribution that the individual narratives about women make to Mark's characterization of discipleship. Their narrative portrayal enhances and extends the definition of discipleship which develops in the portrait of the twelve disciples and offers an additional avenue along which the audience is moved toward embodied virtue.

Markan Discipleship

My intention within this chapter is to outline Mark's broad portrayal of discipleship to clarify how eight women—as a distinct character group within the Gospel—contribute to this thematic emphasis. To create this outline I will first provide a brief summary and analysis of Mark's characterization of the twelve disciples, the character group most readily associated with the contours of Mark's portrayal of discipleship. We will then explore the relationship between the characterization of the women and this broader portrait of the twelve disciples to understand both the women's correspondence with it and their distinction from it. Finally, I will offer a synthetic definition of the concept of narrative discipleship that develops in Mark's Gospel.

FALLIBLE DISCIPLESHIP—THE TWELVE DISCIPLES IN THE GOSPEL OF MARK

One key way that we can consider the concept of discipleship in Mark's Gospel is to examine the narrative portrait of the twelve disciples. Along with Jesus, the twelve disciples function as a major character in the narrative (in contrast to the minor role of the women). They are present in the Gospel from the initial call of four of the disciples (Mark 1:16–20) to Peter's denial of Jesus in the courtyard of the high priest (Mark 14:66–72). Even after their ignominious departure from the story the disciples remain essential characters in Mark's narrative discourse, with the young man at the tomb reiterating Jesus's earlier promise to meet them in Galilee (Mark 16:7). We can gain a significant amount of insight into the nature of discipleship and the way in which the audience may embody its central characteristics by understanding the significance of this particular character group within the wider narrative of Mark's Gospel.

On even a cursory reading of the Gospel, however, it is transparent that Mark's portrait of the twelve disciples is immensely complex. The complexity of their narrative portrait stems from the distinct ways in which the disciples relate to Jesus—the ways in which Mark both "shows" and "tells" them in the narrative. Mark's distinctive characterization of the disciples has led to extensive scholarly discussion concerning the significance of their portrayal, their relationship to Christian history, and their potential impact on both the original and the contemporary audience.[1] My intention

---

1. For an overview of scholarship on the twelve disciples in Mark's Gospel, see esp. Black, *The Disciples according to Mark*; and Skinner, "Study of Character(s)," 3–34.

Part One—Narratives *and* Discipleship

here is to present a more limited discussion of the disciples' portrait as a means to determine the related significance of the individual narratives of women in the Gospel. To that end, I will outline the basic trajectory of the disciples' characterization and its potential function within the wider narrative of the Gospel.

The Trajectory of the Twelve Disciples' Characterization

Studies of the twelve disciples in Mark's Gospel frequently highlight the negative trajectory of their portrayal.[2] As part of the consideration of the way in which Mark develops the theme of discipleship and how the narratives of the women relate to the portrait of the disciples, it will be helpful to provide a basic outline of the way in which the disciples' trajectory develops. In broad terms, within Mark's Gospel the portrait of the disciples develops in four basic stages: (1) their initial call and participation in Jesus's ministry, (2) their turn toward fear and misunderstanding about Jesus's identity and mission, (3) their miscomprehension of Jesus's teaching, and (4) their final abandonment of Jesus.

Mark's initial portrayal of the twelve disciples is predominantly positive. In each of the first three chapters of the Gospel Jesus calls people to join in his ministry and they respond without hesitation—Simon, Andrew, James, and John (Mark 1:16–20), Levi (Mark 2:13–14), and then the entirety of the twelve disciples (Mark 3:13–19). In each of these scenes Jesus either calls or appoints followers to proclaim God's kingdom and to exercise his authority in the world.[3] The two brief summary statements about the disciples' activity in Mark 6:12–13 and 30 point to their effectiveness in participating in the ministry of the kingdom. Further, when other characters in the narrative question aspects of the disciples' behavior Jesus responds by defining their activity in conjunction with the unique nature of his own ministry (Mark 2:18–28; 7:1–23). And, when Jesus's family attempts to interrupt his teaching ministry in Mark 3:20–35, Jesus redefines the language of family with reference specifically to the disciples—"those

---

2. For similar analyses of the negative trajectory of the twelve disciples in Mark's Gospel, see, e.g., Danove, *Rhetoric of Characterization*, 90–126; Garland, *Theology of Mark's Gospel*, 389–433; Hurtado, "Following Jesus," 9–29; Stein, *Mark*, 26–31; Tannehill, "Disciples in Mark," 386–405.

3. On the call narratives, see esp. Henderson, *Christology and Discipleship*, 31–94; and Moloney, "Vocation of the Disciples," esp. 63–83.

Markan Discipleship

seated around him in a circle" (Mark 3:34). In the first stage of Mark's narrative the disciples participate in the ministry of the kingdom and serve primarily as positive exemplars for Mark's audience.

Within this predominantly positive portrayal there are two pieces of evidence which may foreshadow the negative trajectory of the twelve disciples. The first is Mark's concise note that Judas Iscariot betrayed Jesus (Mark 3:19) and the second is the disciples' fearful reaction when Jesus calms the storm on the sea (Mark 4:35-41). Neither of these pieces of evidence, however, clearly demonstrates a negative reading of the disciples in the first instance. The gravity of Judas's betrayal and its connection with the rest of the disciples becomes transparent in Mark 14, but at this earlier stage of the narrative the note of betrayal serves not to tarnish the narrative portrait of the disciples but to distinguish Judas from them. Similarly, the significance of the negative trajectory of Mark's portrayal of the disciples' fearful reaction in the boat only develops as analogous scenes unfold in the narrative. The positive summary of the disciples' ministry in Mark 6 suggests, at least initially, that their dramatic response to Jesus's identity in Mark 4 did not diminish their capacity to participate in the ministry of the kingdom.

As Mark's narrative progresses, however, it becomes clear that the disciples' fearful response to Jesus in Mark 4 functions as a turning point in the trajectory of their narrative portrayal. Mark 4 is the first of three scenes in the narrative which depict an extended interaction between Jesus and the disciples in a boat. Each scene paints an increasingly condemnatory portrait of the disciples' ability to comprehend Jesus's identity and mission. The lack of faith and fear they exhibit in the initial scene (Mark 4:35-41) reverberates in the subsequent boat scenes. In Mark 6:45-52 the disciples experience similar terror as they witness Jesus walk on the water toward them as they struggle to direct their boat against the wind and they mistake him for a ghost (Mark 6:49). Given Mark's emphasis on the unique identity and authority of Jesus in each scene, it may be reasonable to assume that the disciples' fear merely reflects an expected response to an encounter with the divine.[4] In this case, neither scene would require either an immediate rejection of the disciples nor condemnation of their fearful reaction. A more negative evaluation of the disciples in the second scene, however, arises from the narrator's explanation that their fear was the result of the hardened condition of their hearts (Mark 6:52), a note which harks back

---

4. Cf. Judg 6:22-23; Dan 8:17; 10:7, 12; Luke 2:9-10; Rev 1:17.

Part One—Narratives *and* Discipleship

to Jesus's frustration with the hardened hearts of the religious leaders who oppose him (Mark 3:1–5).

The disciples' subsequent encounter with Jesus in a boat in Mark 8:14–21 eliminates any doubt concerning the negative trajectory of Mark's characterization. Here, after twice witnessing Jesus miraculously provide food for a multitude of people (Mark 6:30–44; 8:1–10), the disciples misunderstand Jesus's metaphorical warning about the yeast of the Pharisees and Herod as a reproach for the fact that they had forgotten to bring an adequate supply of bread. Jesus excoriates them for this train of thought, questioning their capacity to perceive, the condition of their hearts, and whether they have eyes to see or ears to hear (Mark 8:17–18). The language of sense perception is particularly acute. It echoes the language of blindness and deafness that characterizes the way those outside of the kingdom perceive Jesus's parables (Mark 4:12). It also creates a stark contrast with the surrounding narratives: the restoration of hearing and speech to the deaf-mute man in the Decapolis (Mark 7:31–37) and the restoration of sight to the blind man at Bethsaida (Mark 8:22–26).[5] In contrast with these two potential outsiders who can now hear and see, the disciples remain confounded about the nature of Jesus's identity and ministry. The portrait of the disciples that develops in the first major section of Mark's Gospel (Mark 1:1–8:21) is marked by tension. They are neither wholly positive exemplars nor completely negative antagonists.

The complex nature of Mark's characterization of the twelve disciples continues as the narrative progresses in Mark 8:22—10:52. This section of the Gospel constitutes the most extensive focus on Jesus's teaching in the Markan narrative, with a particular focus on defining the relationship between Jesus's ministry and the nature of discipleship. Jesus's teaching on discipleship develops through three predictions of his death and resurrection (Mark 8:31; 9:31; 10:32–34). After each prediction the disciples respond in overtly negative ways—with insolence (Mark 8:32–33), fearful silence (Mark 9:32), and misplaced arrogance (Mark 10:35–41). In connection with the portrait of fear and misperception that develops in the earlier boat scenes, the disciples' initial positive portrayal fades extensively as they fail to coordinate their own actions and ideals with those of Jesus. It is crucial to note, however, that each instance of failed comprehension by the disciples is followed by a dramatic description of the obligations of discipleship—cruciformity (Mark 8:34–38), inversion of social hierarchies

---

5. Tannehill, "Disciples in Mark," 399–400; cf. Strauss, *Mark*, 745.

Markan Discipleship

(Mark 9:35-37), and self-sacrificial service (Mark 10:42-45). Each of the three passion-resurrection predictions, therefore, exhibits a rhetorical pattern that connects Jesus's predictions with an instance of discipleship failure and a subsequent call to a reimagined form of discipleship.[6] Because of this rhetorical pattern, the disciples continue to function as exemplars with respect to the discourse of the narrative even as their portrait within the story of the narrative continues to devolve. Each instance of the disciples' failure provides an opportunity for Jesus to define a form of discipleship ordered around his own identity and mission.

The disciples' negative trajectory reaches its nadir in Mark 14. In the initial stages of the passion narrative Jesus predicts the betrayal of Judas (Mark 14:17-20), the desertion of the disciples (Mark 14:27), and Peter's threefold rejection (Mark 14:30). Despite Peter's emphatic assertion of continued solidarity and the disciples' vigorous protestations against Jesus's prediction, each of the events takes place accordingly in the narrative. Judas leads the commissioned mob to the garden to arrest Jesus (Mark 14:43-45), the disciples flee the scene in dramatic and shameful fashion (Mark 14:50-52), and Peter denies having even known who Jesus was (Mark 14:66-72). Peter's vehement denials evoke Jesus's stark warning to those who reject the cruciform demands of discipleship: "whoever is ashamed of me and my words in this adulterous and sinful generation, the Son of Man will be ashamed of them" (Mark 8:38).[7] The net effect is remarkable. Those who had followed Jesus without hesitation and joined him in the ministry of God's in-breaking kingdom now refuse to admit that they may even have known him tangentially.

There are at least two pieces of evidence in Mark 13-16, however, that make the disciples' downward trajectory somewhat less precipitous. First, the eschatological discourse in Mark 13 presumes the disciples' future participation in the ministry of Jesus. Jesus's warnings against false teachers (Mark 13:5-8) and his description of the disciples' future suffering (Mark 13:9-11) are both conditioned on the reality of the disciples' ongoing engagement in kingdom ministry.[8] Second, the young man's instruction to the women at the tomb to tell the disciples that Jesus would meet them in Gali-

---

6. On Mark's development of this pattern, see, e.g., Gorman, *Death of the Messiah*, 87; Hays, *Moral Vision*, 80-85; Hurtado, "Following Jesus," 11-15; Schüssler Fiorenza, *In Memory of Her*, 317; Tannehill, "Disciples in Mark," 400-401.

7. Cf. Tannehill, "Disciples in Mark," 402.

8. Hurtado, "Following Jesus," 22; Malbon, "Text and Contexts," 91.

lee (Mark 16:7) anticipates their future reconciliation.⁹ The abandonment in Gethsemane is overcome in the return to Galilee.

The Function of the Twelve Disciples' Characterization

Approaching Mark's Gospel as a theological and aretegenic narrative—an act of communication between author and audience which seeks to transform—requires that we offer an explanation for the complex and predominantly negative characterization of the twelve disciples. In what way does Mark's narrative portrayal of this group move the audience toward the formation of virtue? Elizabeth Struthers Malbon's extensive work on characters and characterization in Mark's Gospel is instructive at this point.¹⁰ In particular, her designation of the disciples as "fallible followers" provides a helpful construct for understanding the narrative complexity of their portrayal, both in terms of their individual characterization and their relationship to other participants in the narrative (e.g., Jesus and the women).¹¹ Recognizing that the disciples are neither solely positive exemplars nor completely negative antagonists allows for a more flexible description of their narrative function.

One of the constructive dimensions of Malbon's use of the language of fallibility is its compatibility with the paradigm of characterization developed by Cornelis Bennema which seeks to describe characters along a continuum of complexity that accounts for the dynamic functions they may have within a narrative (see ch. 1). To describe the twelve disciples merely as flat or round, major or minor, or positive or negative, would fail to account for the diverse nature of their portrayal and function within Mark's wider narrative world. Malbon's language of fallibility avoids this rhetorical pitfall by providing space for a more nuanced analysis of the disciples' characterization. The disciples' narrative portrait is not conditioned by a single emphasis or a single trajectory. The positive aspects of their portrayal that appear prior to and within their broadly negative trajectory point to their development within the progression of the narrative and, consequently, to the multiplicity of their narrative functions.

The tension in Mark's characterization of the disciples is an essential aspect of the way in which the narrative communicates to the audience not

---

9. Malbon, "Text and Contexts," 91.
10. See esp. the collected essays in Malbon, *In the Company of Jesus*.
11. Malbon, "Fallible Followers," 29–48; cf. Hurtado, "Following Jesus," 21–23.

Markan Discipleship

a detriment to it. The rounded complexity of the disciples' characterization creates a framework in which the audience may engage with and respond to their narrative portrait in a number of ways. As Malbon notes:

> Hope and critique, identification and judgment, are not direct opposites. "Identification with" characters is not simply equivalent to "admiration of" them, and "judgment of" a character group does not necessarily mean "dissociation from" it.... The key issue for the implied audience is *not* identification with positive characters versus dissociation from negative characters ... but developing sympathy, empathy and community particularly with the paradoxical characters within a range of characters and character groups.[12]

In other words, the complex portrait of the twelve disciples suggests that the audience's response will be equally complex. Audiences of Mark's Gospel can embody the immediate willingness of the disciples to follow Jesus. They can participate as the disciples did in proclaiming the in-breaking of God's kingdom. They can reject the disciples' fear and misunderstanding concerning Jesus's identity and mission. They can take up the radical demands of discipleship which the disciples initially fail to personify. They can remain unashamed of the Son of Man even when facing personal and social rejection.

As we noted in the previous chapter, characters are deployed in Mark's Gospel to support the theological agenda of the narrative. Mark's complex characterization of the disciples is conditioned by his wider aim to describe the good news about Jesus that reshapes the trajectory of human history (including the trajectory of the disciples). The distinct relationship that the disciples have with Jesus—especially as it develops in the key texts that link Jesus's own ministry with the definition of discipleship and examples of the disciples' unmitigated failure (Mark 8:31–38; 9:30–37; 10:32–45)—demonstrates their position as those through whom Mark can characterize the complex nature of discipleship itself. To return again to the insightful analysis of Malbon:

> followership *is* characterized in Mark as involving the lively struggle between faith and doubt, trust and fear, obedience and

---

12. Malbon, "Minor Characters," 63 (emphasis original). See also Garland, *Theology of Mark's Gospel*, 406: "Mark does not intend for readers to be merely observers who look disdainfully at the disciples' ineptitude but to identify with them and recognize their own inadequacies as disciples and be moved to correct them."

Part One—Narratives *and* Discipleship

denial. . . . Mark wishes to show who Jesus is and who Jesus' followers are. To do this he schematizes the characters of his story; he paints extreme cases of enemies and exemplars as the background against which the trials and joys of followers may stand out more boldly. If Mark's Gospel is in any sense a polemic, it is a polemic . . . against a simplistic view of discipleship (or followership) that sees unfailing support or unfailing enmity as the only options, rather than as the background against which the complex relations of Jesus and his followers must be worked out.[13]

To frame this idea in the language of narrative criticism, although the "story" of the disciples moves along a predominantly negative trajectory, the "discourse" of the disciples draws the audience's attention to their role in the narrative as respondents to Jesus—both in their submission to him and in their rejection of him. The intent of Mark's portrayal of the disciples is not to get us to respond directly to the *disciples*. The intent is to encourage us to respond to *Jesus*. Indeed, the primary way that we are able to evaluate the disciples and to discern how to respond to them is by evaluating them in relationship to Jesus and by responding to Jesus. To modify the language Suzanne Watts Henderson uses in the conclusion of her study on the relationship between Christology and discipleship in Mark's Gospel, once the entire narrative is in view it becomes clear that faithful discipleship entails both a correct appraisal of Jesus's christological identity and a collective participation in Jesus's christological mission.[14] Moving the audience along this christological trajectory is the main function of Mark's complex portrayal of the twelve disciples.

Jesus is the central character around which Mark's narrative revolves and the only true paradigm from which discipleship develops.[15] Both the concord and the contradiction that develop in the interaction between Jesus and the twelve disciples provides the narrative space in which Mark portrays the nature and obligations of discipleship. This narrative space is then extended in Mark's portrayal of the way in which other characters

---

13. Malbon, "Jewish Leaders," 279 (emphasis original).

14. Henderson, *Christology and Discipleship*, 241.

15. So Best, *Following Jesus*; Hurtado, "Following Jesus," 25–27. On Mark's intentional presentation of Jesus, see esp. Boring, "Markan Christology," 451–71; Broadhead, *Naming Jesus*; Danove, *Rhetoric of Characterization*; Davidsen, *Narrative Jesus*; Kingsbury, *Christology of Mark's Gospel*; Malbon, *Mark's Jesus*; Morrison, *Turning Point in the Gospel of Mark*; Naluparayil, *Identity of Jesus in Mark*; Tannehill, "Gospel of Mark as Narrative Christology," 57–95.

Markan Discipleship

engage with and respond to Jesus. The Jewish leaders, the crowds, and the minor characters all provide insight into Mark's portrait of discipleship. Mark's creative, diverse, and intentional use of characters compels the audience to reflect deeply on the nuanced portrait of discipleship that develops in the progression of the narrative. The intent of Mark's varied use of characterization is not merely to force a rejection of certain sets of characters and an acceptance of others, but rather an identification—whether positively or negatively, approvingly or disapprovingly—with the complex spectrum of characters and the traits they embody.[16] It is within this wider spectrum of characterization that the characteristics of discipleship necessitated by God's in-breaking kingdom in Jesus unfold.

FAITHFUL DISCIPLESHIP—WOMEN AS DISCIPLES IN THE GOSPEL OF MARK

One of the key segments of this characterization spectrum is Mark's portrayal of women.[17] Mark narrates key engagements between Jesus and women to emphasize particular qualities of discipleship. In spite of the fact that the narrative space in which the women reside is significantly smaller than that of the twelve disciples, Mark uses their concise narratives to identify specific characteristics of discipleship more sharply. Although there are some who argue that Mark intentionally suppresses the role of women, the general consensus among Markan scholars is that certain women are portrayed as exemplary figures in the narrative.[18] The bleeding woman (Mark 5:25–34), the Syrophoenician woman (Mark 7:24–30), the poor widow (Mark 12:41–44), and the woman who anoints Jesus (Mark 14:3–9) are often held up alongside other minor characters such as Jairus (Mark 5:21–24; 35–43) and Bartimaeus (Mark 10:46–52) as those who embody key aspects of what it means to be a faithful follower of Jesus.[19] At the very least the

---

16. Malbon, "Minor Characters," 63.

17. For book-length treatments of the women in Mark's Gospel, see Fander, *Die Stellung der Frau im Markusevangelium*; Kinukawa, *Women and Jesus in Mark*; Miller, *Women in Mark's Gospel*; Mitchell, *Beyond Fear and Silence*.

18. For the argument that Mark intentionally suppresses the women, see Munro, "Women Disciples in Mark?" 225–41. On the question of why the Gospel authors never explicitly refer to women as disciples, see Meier, *Companions and Competitors*, 73–80.

19. See, e.g., Beavis, "Women as Models of Faith," 3–9; Edwards, *Mark*, 417; Malbon, "Fallible Followers," 36–40; Miller, "Women Characters," 174–93; Swartley, "Role of Women," 16–22; Tetlow, *Women and Ministry*, 94–98; Williams, *Other Followers*,

Part One—Narratives *and* Discipleship

individual narratives of these women contribute to Mark's presentation of Jesus.

There is also a general consensus, however, that Mark's broadly positive portrayal of the women eventually follows the same negative trajectory along which the portrait of the twelve disciples declines. Whereas certain anonymous women in Mark 1–14 embody key characteristics of Jesus's ministry, the named women who enter the narrative in Mark 15–16 abandon Jesus, fleeing the tomb in fearful silence and failing to fulfill their commission to proclaim to the disciples that the crucified one is risen (Mark 16:6–8).[20] Further, as with the portrayal of the twelve disciples, Mark's characterization of female characters does not follow a single trajectory from positive to negative. Prior to the introduction of the named women in Mark 15–16, there are other scenes which shift the trajectory in different ways. Herodias and her daughter are ostensibly negative characters in their conspiracy against John the Baptist (Mark 6:14–29). Jesus's mother and sisters are portrayed at best as neutral toward him when they attempt to take charge of him in Galilee (Mark 3:31–35; 6:3).[21] And the servant girl plays a contrarian role in the narrative in her interrogation of Peter in the courtyard of the high priest during Jesus's trial (Mark 14:66–72).[22] The trajectory of Mark's portrayal of the women reflects the same type of complexity as that of the twelve disciples.

Given the diversity of their portraits it may be most constructive to follow Malbon in describing Mark's characterization of the women with the more nuanced language of fallibility. Mark does not create a strict contrast with respect to the gender of the two character groups—the men as failures and the women as exemplars of the characteristics of Jesus's identity and mission. As with the twelve disciples, the overall portrait of the women highlights characteristics both amenable and antagonistic to Mark's narrative presentation of Jesus.[23] Because of this, Mark's characterization of the women is not intended to stand in conflict with the characterization of

---

112–21, 176–82.

20. See esp. Lincoln, "Promise and the Failure," 283–300; cf. Boring, *Mark*, 448–49; Hooker, *Mark*, 387; Moloney, *Gospel of Mark*, 348–54.

21. For a more negative assessment of Jesus's mother and sisters, see Miller, *Women in Mark's Gospel*, 33–38.

22. Mark's characterization of two further women, the daughters of Jairus and the Syrophoenician woman, is not extensive, though both are recipients of dramatic acts of restoration. On the place of daughters in Mark's narrative, see Betsworth, *Reign of God*.

23. Malbon, "Fallible Followers," 33, 46.

the twelve disciples. Any narrative tension that exists between the groups stems not from direct conflict between them or in the distinction in their genders but from the distinct ways in which their narrative portraits relate to Jesus.[24] Both the negative and the exemplary characteristics that Mark emphasizes in the narratives of certain women may also be gleaned from the narratives of the twelve disciples and other minor characters. Mark's wider presentation of Jesus develops both in the way in which he "shows" and "tells" Jesus and in the way in which he "shows" and "tells" Jesus in relation to other characters, the women included.

Although I find the language of fallibility to be constructive as a general description of the nuanced portrait of disciples and discipleship in Mark's narrative, I want to propose that Mark's characterization of certain women in the narrative creates a distinct portrait of faithfulness. More specifically, by employing the concept of narrative analogy I want to argue that Mark creates an intentional pattern of faithful discipleship through the connection of the narratives of eight women in the Gospel. Mark's characterization of Simon's mother-in-law (Mark 1:29–31), the bleeding woman (Mark 5:25–34), the Syrophoenician woman (Mark 7:24–30), the poor widow (Mark 12:41–44), the woman who anoints Jesus (Mark 14:3–9), and the three named women in the passion narrative (Mark 15:40–41, 47; 16:1–8) deliberately integrates them into a character group whose narratives can be interpreted in light of one another. The inclusion of Simon's mother-in-law and the named women is crucial for the development of this pattern. The individual narratives of these women establish the continuity of the pattern throughout the entire progression of the Gospel. Further, that the women in Mark 15–16 function as the culmination of this narrative pattern

---

24. Within Mark's narrative the only direct interactions between the women and the twelve disciples are Simon's mother-in-law's act of service to them (Mark 1:29–31) and the young woman's interrogation of Peter during Jesus's trial (Mark 14:66–72). While the young woman's interrogation is significant for the progression of Mark's portrayal of Peter, it does not provide any specific insight into her own response to Jesus. In contrast to Matthew's portrait of the Canaanite woman (Matt 15:21–28), Mark does not portray any comment by the disciples in the narrative of the Syrophoenician woman (Mark 7:24–30). Additionally, Mark does not identify those who complain about the woman's waste of resources in anointing Jesus (Mark 14:4), whereas Matthew identifies them as the disciples (Matt 26:8–9) and John specifically names Judas (John 12:4–5). Mark narrates the final instruction given to the women to speak to the disciples without any description of the nature of the interaction (Mark 16:7–8), whereas Luke portrays the general disbelief of the disciples (Luke 24:11–12).

Part One—Narratives *and* Discipleship

constitutes a distinct reading of Mark's Gospel.[25] I will argue in chapter 6 that the women's departure from the tomb is not an act of abandonment (fallibility) but a fulfillment of their specific commission and a narrative representation of discipleship (faithfulness). The outcome of the integration of the narratives of these women is a unique portrait that contributes to Mark's narrative development of what it means to be a faithful follower of Jesus and an embodied participant in God's kingdom.

In different ways these eight women function as narrative embodiments of essential aspects of God's in-breaking kingdom—restored life, kingdom speech, sacrificial action, and cruciformity. These characteristics are essential because they are rooted in Mark's wider narrative about the life, death, and resurrection of Jesus. That the narratives of these women are related to Jesus is essential in light of the reality that the only adequate paradigm for discipleship in Mark's Gospel is Jesus himself. The theological impact of the women's narratives is defined by their relationship to Jesus.[26] The women's demonstration of these specific characteristics of discipleship is an example of what Malbon refers to as "reflected" Christology. The women are small but polished mirrors that reflect crucial aspects of Mark's portrayal of Jesus.[27]

In his seminal essay on Mark's Christology, Robert Tannehill argues that the narrative shape of the Gospel needs to condition the way we think about Mark's presentation of the identity and mission of Jesus. For Tannehill, Mark's Gospel itself is an act of "narrative Christology."[28] Importantly, Tannehill asserts that:

> Our understanding of these matters is enriched by study of the role relationships among Jesus and others in the story, which sometimes involve reiterative enrichment and sometimes unexpected development. The author guides his readers' response to the story by narrative patterns which control emphasis and the evaluation of events and characters.[29]

---

25. For a positive interpretation of the women in Mark 15–16, see Aernie, "Cruciform Discipleship," 779–97; Bauckham, *Gospel Women*, 286–95; Hurtado, "Women, the Tomb," 427–50.

26. Malbon, "Fallible Followers," 46; cf. Hurtado, "Following Jesus," 25.

27. Malbon, "Reflected Christology," 127–45; cf. Malbon, *Mark's Jesus*, 219–30.

28. Tannehill, "Gospel of Mark as Narrative Christology," 89.

29. Ibid., 88–89.

Markan Discipleship

The rhetorical connection of the individual narratives of these women is, I believe, an example of the type of narrative pattern that Tannehill identifies. Through the use of narrative analogy Mark draws the attention of the audience to a character group that exhibits a form of faithfulness that shapes their position with respect to Jesus and to the rest of his followers. The narrative shape of the Gospel, therefore, must also condition the way we think about Mark's presentation of the identity and mission of Jesus's followers. The integrated narratives of the women are an example of the way in which the Gospel is also an act of narrative discipleship.

NARRATIVE DISCIPLESHIP IN THE GOSPEL OF MARK

The theological and aretegenic emphases of Mark's Gospel develop not systematically, but narratively. Mark's emphasis on the way in which God's kingdom breaks into the world through the life, death, and resurrection of Jesus develops through the plot of his story—its settings, events, and characters. The impact of God's in-breaking kingdom is neither enumerated in a list of specific characteristics nor relayed through a distinct summary of its components. The theological impact of the narrative stems from the progression of the narrative itself and so has to be discerned from an engagement with the narrative itself. One of the key ways in which this engagement arises is through Mark's intentional portrayal of characters and the relational intersections between them. Through the development of these portraits the audience gains a distinct entry point into the narrative and can learn to follow the direction of its theological trajectory.

Without question Jesus is the central character in the Gospel. The entire narrative revolves around the good news that originates from Jesus and extends out from him in his ministry and passion. This good news is defined by the reality that God's kingdom is now emphatically present in Jesus (Mark 1:14–15). The way in which Mark portrays Jesus provides insight into what the nature of this kingdom is. Jesus's acts of restoration, his proclamation of the kingdom, his holistic sacrifice on the cross, and God's vindication of him in his death and resurrection all give shape to this new kingdom reality. This distinctly christological focus of Mark's narrative not only provides information about the historical and theological realities of Jesus, it also creates the paradigm that Mark's audience is called to embody. As an act of communication the narrative of the Gospel intends to both inform and transform. Mark's intentionally crafted narrative is a dynamic

Part One—Narratives *and* Discipleship

entity with theological intent. Through the way Mark presents his narrative Christology he creates narrative discipleship.

Narrative discipleship refers to the composite set of actions and attributes associated with the identity of Jesus and derived from the cruciform shape of his life and ministry which Mark portrays in the Gospel as essential for those who desire to participate in the reality of God's in-breaking kingdom. Both Mark's specific presentation of Jesus and his portrayal of the way in which other characters interact with him creates the narrative framework in which this composite set of actions and attributes develops. As we have seen, the complex portrait of the twelve disciples and their engagement with Jesus provides extensive insight into the shape of what it means to be a follower of Jesus. The disciples' characterization emphasizes the need for unconditional obedience (Mark 1:16–20), proclamation of the kingdom (Mark 3:14), cruciformity (Mark 8:34–38), the inversion of social hierarchies (Mark 9:35–37), self-sacrificial service (Mark 10:42–45), and prayerful watchfulness (Mark 13:5).[30] But even these essential characteristics are not the sum total of Mark's definition of discipleship. The portrait of the disciples is not the only aspect of the narrative which offers insight into the shape of the kingdom and the nature of discipleship.

As Joel Williams so aptly notes, "Mark's portrayal of the disciples may be the logical place to start an investigation of discipleship in Mark's Gospel, but it would be an improper place to end such a study."[31] Mark's development of the theme of discipleship is enhanced through Jesus's engagement with other narrative figures. The aim of the present volume is to detail how Mark intentionally uses a specific set of eight women to provide further substance to the theme of discipleship and to construct another mirror in which the audience is able to see ways in which it might reflect the identity and ministry of Jesus. As a character group these women serve as narrative representations of four essential components of Markan discipleship— restored life (Mark 1:29–31; 5:25–34), kingdom speech (Mark 7:24–30), sacrificial action (Mark 12:41–44; 14:3–9), and cruciformity (Mark 15–16). The exegetical chapters in part two aim to describe more fully how the individual narratives of these women extend the portrait of narrative discipleship in which the audience of the Gospel is drawn to participate.

---

30. For itemized lists of the characteristics of discipleship in Mark's Gospel, see Bayer, *Theology of Mark*, 99–124; and Garland, *Theology of Mark's Gospel*, 439–54.

31. Williams, *Other Followers*, 205.

CONCLUSION

The purpose of this chapter was to provide an introduction to the theme of Markan discipleship. I began by examining Mark's characterization of the twelve disciples. The complex trajectory of the narrative of the disciples provides a broad foundation for Mark's wider portrayal of discipleship. This foundation stems not directly from the disciples themselves, but from their interaction—both positive and negative, expected and unexpected—with Jesus. It is the disciples' reflection of the christological trajectory of Mark's Gospel that gives their characterization significance for it is only in the life, death, and resurrection of Jesus that the paradigm of discipleship is created. I then offered a concise introduction to Mark's portrayal of the women. Although the narrative presence of the women is more constricted than that of the disciples, their narratives serve to emphasize elements of the wider narrative more sharply. Like the twelve disciples, Mark's characterization of the women is complex. Certain women are antagonistic toward Jesus. Others extend the boundaries of Mark's portrait of discipleship. In particular, I argued that Mark crafts the narratives of eight women to broaden his portrait of discipleship. Mark's intentional integration of the narratives of these women in the Gospel contributes to what I refer to as narrative discipleship—the composite set of actions and attributes associated with the identity of Jesus and derived from the cruciform shape of his life and ministry which Mark portrays in the Gospel as essential for those who desire to participate in the reality of God's in-breaking kingdom.

Part Two—Narratives *of* Discipleship

3

Restored Discipleship (Mark 1 and 5)

INTRODUCTION

GOD'S KINGDOM BRINGS ABOUT the re-creation and restoration of the world. Perhaps the clearest examples in Mark's Gospel of this theological reality are the portrayals of Jesus's power to heal. There are a number of healing narratives in Mark's Gospel that display Jesus's authority over sickness and death (e.g., Mark 1:29–34, 40–45; 2:1–12; 3:1–5; 5:21–43; 7:24–36; 8:22–26; 9:14–29; 10:46–52). There is a clear emphasis at these points in Mark's narrative on Jesus's identity, power, and mission. But to focus only on their christological dimensions would neglect the wider impact of these stories in the Gospel. Jesus not only heals, *people are healed*. Mark portrays real, physical restoration in these narratives. The aim of this chapter is to discuss the way in which these healing narratives relate to Mark's wider development of the theme of discipleship. In light of the aretegenic dimension of the Gospel, it is important to recognize that Mark's healing narratives not only provide information about Christology but also impact the way in which the audience responds to the narrative. These scenes of restoration help to define the nature of what it means to be a disciple of Jesus.

In this chapter I want to focus on two particular instances of healing—Jesus's restoration of Simon's mother-in-law (Mark 1:29–31) and his restoration of the woman who suffers from chronic bleeding (Mark 5:25–34). These are not the only two women who are restored by Jesus in Mark's

Part Two—Narratives *of* Discipleship

narrative. He also heals the daughters of both Jairus (Mark 5:21–24, 35–43) and the Syrophoenician woman (Mark 7:24–30). The narratives of Simon's mother-in-law and the bleeding woman, however, offer more developed portraits of each woman's interaction with Jesus. In contrast, the revivification of Jairus's daughter results in her moving around but not explicitly interacting with Jesus, while the healing of the daughter of the Syrophoenician woman happens from a distance, with Jesus never encountering the girl in Mark's narrated story. This is not to suggest that either daughter is unimportant in Mark's narrative. Both their stories and that of their faithful parents play crucial roles in the development of Mark's Christology and the wider portrait of discipleship. Nevertheless, the specific focus of this chapter is on the way in which two of Jesus's acts of restoration function within Mark's wider presentation of discipleship.

My intention within this chapter is to describe how the portraits of these two women contribute to the definition of what it means to be a follower of Jesus. In other words, we want to develop an answer to the following question: how do these women function as narrative exemplars of Markan discipleship? The suggestion that I want to put forward is that these two narratives develop portraits of *restored discipleship*. The engagement that these two women have with Jesus provides insight into the way in which Jesus's restorative agency shapes and defines the lives of those who follow him. In particular, the way in which the women respond to Jesus in light of their restored condition constitutes an initial aspect of Mark's wider development of narrative discipleship. To develop this thesis we will look first at the healing of Simon's mother-in-law (Mark 1:29–31) and then work through the narrative of the bleeding woman (Mark 5:25–34).

SIMON'S MOTHER-IN-LAW (MARK 1:29–31)

Jesus's healing of Simon's mother-in-law occurs as part of a series of short vignettes at the beginning of the Gospel. Jesus is introduced by John the Baptist, baptized, thrust into a period of temptation in the wilderness, and then enters into Galilee proclaiming the arrival of God's kingdom and the need for repentance and belief. The proclamation of the message is immediately put into action—Jesus calls four disciples (Simon, Andrew, James, and John) who then accompany him to Capernaum where he begins to teach in the synagogue, is confronted by a man with an evil spirit, and consequently performs an exorcism. The rapid-fire nature of Mark's narrative

Restored Discipleship (Mark 1 and 5)

continues as Jesus and the disciples leave the synagogue and immediately enter into the house of Simon and Andrew.[1] Certain people present in the house inform Jesus that Simon's mother-in-law is confined to bed with a fever, to which he responds with an immediate act of healing. The preceding exorcism and Jesus's healing of Simon's mother-in-law then become the catalyst for a significant number of sick and demon-possessed people being brought to Jesus so that he might provide them with physical restoration.

Restored Life

There is an important connection throughout Mark's narrative between sickness and demonic activity.[2] Although the two realities are never strictly related, it is clear that part of the redemptive process of Jesus's ministry involves an overturning of both of these realities of humanity's broken existence. One of the essential ideas that Mark develops in the Gospel is that God acts in Jesus to bring about a kingdom that overturns the broken reality of the present age and inaugurates a renewed creation.[3] Susan Miller argues that Mark's portrayal of this divine act of new creation is particularly present in the narratives that involve women.[4] Although Miller presses this aspect of her study too far at certain points, she is certainly correct that there is an emphasis in Mark's narrative on the theme of new creation and the related reality of restoration. As Miller notes, "the healing of Simon's mother-in-law forms a paradigm of Jesus' power to raise humanity. Jesus not only liberates human beings from disease but has the power to raise them from death."[5]

Although this note of restoration is more frequently associated with the revivification of Jairus's daughter (Mark 5:21–24, 35–43) and Jesus's own resurrection (Mark 16:6), Miller's connection between the narrative of Simon's mother-in-law and the theme of restoration is not an exegetical

---

1. Archaeological evidence from Capernaum shows the close geographical proximity in the first century CE between a synagogue and a home that seems to have been used for early Christian gatherings. For the argument that this is potentially the house owned by Simon and Andrew, see Strange and Shanks, "House Where Jesus Stayed," 26–37.

2. Marcus, *Mark*, 1:199.

3. For an introduction to the "apocalyptic" and "cosmic" categories in Mark's narrative, see ibid., 1:71–73.

4. Miller, *Women in Mark's Gospel*.

5. Ibid., 22.

Part Two — Narratives *of* Discipleship

overstatement. In spite of the fact that modern medical practices have helped us control what we refer to as fevers, within the ancient world a fever was not merely a symptom of another sickness but a life-threatening condition in its own right.⁶ Jesus's restorative action in the present context is not merely the divine equivalent of the application of a cool compress. It is, rather, an act of real restoration. Jesus takes hold of (κρατήσας) Simon's mother-in-law, raises her (ἤγειρεν αὐτήν) out of a critical situation, and provides her with restored life (Mark 1:31).

Mark's assertion that Jesus "raised her," is both expected in the immediate domestic context—she is laying down (Mark 1:30)—and connected with a number of other healing narratives in which the same language is used (e.g., Mark 2:9, 11; 3:3; 10:49), especially that of the healing of the deaf and mute boy in Mark 9:14–29: "Jesus grasped him (κρατήσας) by his hand and raised him (ἤγειρεν)" (Mark 9:27; cf. 5:41). Mark's use of "raised" may also evoke a correspondence with his use of the same vocabulary to describe Jesus's own resurrection (Mark 14:28; 16:6).⁷ Even if these narrative connections remain somewhat tenuous, I believe Miller is still accurate in her assessment of the importance of this portion of the Gospel for Mark's wider portrait of Jesus. Jesus's ministry inaugurates the new creation—it involves divine restoration and creates restored disciples.⁸

Restored Characterization

It would not be constructive to attempt to establish an entire framework for narrative discipleship upon the small foundation of Mark's portrait of the healing of Simon's mother-in-law. At its most basic point this is a narrative example of Jesus's restorative power. His embodiment of the message about God's kingdom results in a reordering of creation in which the brokenness of the fallen human condition is transformed. The good news of Mark's Gospel is that the reality of the new creation is indeed taking place in and through Jesus. The full implications of Jesus's restorative power and authority, however, are not developed in this short scene. Indeed, the preceding narrative of Jesus's exorcism in the synagogue at Capernaum (Mark 1:21–28) already hints at the fact that a complete portrait of Jesus's identity will

---

6. See, e.g., Black, *Mark*, 75; Boring, *Mark*, 66; Donahue and Harrington, *Gospel of Mark*, 84.

7. Black refers to the potential connection as the "faintest whisper" (*Mark*, 75).

8. Cf. Miller, *Women in Mark's Gospel*, 27.

Restored Discipleship (Mark 1 and 5)

only emerge in the subsequent narrative. It is only in the climax of Mark's Gospel that Jesus's identity comes to the forefront, first in the centurion's proclamation at the cross that Jesus is the son of God (Mark 15:39) and, second, in the young man's declaration at the tomb that the crucified one is risen (Mark 16:6). The early narrative of Jesus's healing of Simon's mother-in-law constitutes a small sample of the wider reality of Jesus's identity and its implications.

It would be equally unhelpful, however, to swing the pendulum too far in the other direction by assuming that the brevity of this section of the Gospel makes it insignificant in the structure and development of Mark's wider narrative. On the contrary, there are at least two aspects of the narrative that speak to its importance in the wider Gospel: (1) the reality of the woman's minor role in the narrative and (2) that her immediate response is one of service. Simon's mother-in-law is significant for the development of the narrative because she is not featured again in the narrative. That initial point may seem somewhat counterintuitive. In her important essay on characterization in Mark's Gospel, however, Elizabeth Struthers Malbon demonstrates that Mark frequently uses minor characters—those characters who lack a recurring presence in the narrated story—to demonstrate exemplary aspects of discipleship.[9] In addition to the other women discussed in the present volume, who are all minor characters, the exemplary function of minor characters is also developed in narratives like those of Bartimaeus (Mark 10:46–52) and Simon of Cyrene (Mark 15:21). The narrative of Simon's mother-in-law is one example of a larger rhetorical device that Mark employs to create a spectrum of responses to Jesus's ministry. What becomes clear throughout Mark's narrative is that one of the primary purposes of a number of female characters is to demonstrate a positive response to Jesus.

During a first hearing of Mark's Gospel this wider narrative function of the story about Simon's mother-in-law would likely not have been immediately transparent. In its own context it is primarily an introduction to the restorative power of Jesus that is also demonstrated in the preceding exorcism of the evil spirit (Mark 1:21–28) and in the immediately following summary of Jesus's many healings and exorcisms (Mark 1:32–34). Within the wider development of the narrative, however, the story of this healed woman becomes structurally linked with the narratives of the other women

---

9. Malbon, "Minor Characters," 58–86; cf. Williams, *Other Followers*. See also the discussion of minor characters in ch. 1.

Part Two—Narratives *of* Discipleship

in light of their analogous content. Two important caveats need to be noted at this stage. This woman's positive function in the narrative as an exemplar of discipleship is conditioned solely neither by her position as a minor character in the narrative nor by her gender. There are minor characters in the narrative that are clearly not exemplars of discipleship. For example, the rich man in Mark 10:17–31 retreats from the demands involved in following Jesus. The function of characters in the Gospel is determined not by the frequency with which they appear but rather by their engagement with Jesus within the context of their own narratives. The gender of specific characters is also not necessarily demonstrative of their relationship to Jesus.[10] Even though the present volume is focused on developing a construct of Markan discipleship through the lens of female exemplars, this does not mean that Markan discipleship is gendered. There is an important *pattern* in Mark's narrative in which women are frequently portrayed as embodying essential characteristics of discipleship, but this is not a strict *paradigm*.

Returning to the narrative of Simon's mother-in-law we can see both of these caveats at work. At this early stage of Mark's Gospel it would be nearly impossible for the audience to know that minor characters were going to serve frequently as positive exemplars in the narrative. That will only become clear as the rest of the narrative develops and we are able to see the minor characters in relation to each other. Likewise, that her gender will form part of the larger pattern of narrative discipleship in the Gospel becomes clear only when subsequent stories of women also contribute to the progression of Mark's wider narrative of Jesus. Apart from these two caveats, the way in which this woman's positive valuation develops within the context of her own narrative is through her engagement with Jesus after she becomes the beneficiary of his restorative power. It is her service that is the primary characteristic of her discipleship.

Restored Service

Given the domestic setting of the narrative, the woman's response to the absence of her fever—"she served them" (διηκόνει αὐτοῖς; Mark 1:31)—is frequently understood as a reference to domestic activity, the preparation and service of a meal. R. T. France is representative of one section of Markan scholarship when he says that: "While διακονέω [service] has a wide range of meaning, in this context its basic sense of domestic provision

10. See esp. Malbon, "Fallible Followers," 29–48.

Restored Discipleship (Mark 1 and 5)

seems most likely; she fulfilled what would have been the expected role of the mother-in-law in the family home, by serving up refreshments."[11] France and others are certainly correct that in the immediate context of the narrative the service in which the woman participates is a form of domestic service. More important than the specific nature of the service, however, is what the service represents in both the immediate context and the wider narrative of Mark's Gospel. With respect to the immediate context of the narrative, the woman's service reflects the comprehensive reality of her restoration. In the words of Eugene Boring, "she is now restored to the fullness of life."[12] Mark highlights her service not as a means of categorizing the nature of her response as appropriate to her cultural or gendered position but as a means of clarifying the reality of her status as a restored human. In the same way that the healed paralytic is able to carry his bed (Mark 2:12) and Jairus's daughter is able to walk and eat (Mark 5:42-43), the woman confirms the reality of her restoration through her active service.[13]

The brief description of the woman's service also plays a larger role in the wider context of Mark's narrative. The verb that Mark uses to describe the woman's service (διακονέω) functions later in the narrative as a key term for the nature of discipleship.[14] This specific term is used five times in the Gospel. Prior to its use in the present scene, the term is first used in Mark 1:13, where it describes the way in which the angels serve Jesus during his time in the wilderness. After these two initial occurrences in the early stages of the Gospel, the verb does not appear again until it occurs twice in Mark 10:45 as part of one of Jesus's programmatic statements about the nature of his ministry: "For even the Son of Man did not come to be served (διακονηθῆναι), but to serve (διακονῆσαι), and to give his life as a ransom for many." That Jesus's statement is also an implicit exhortation about the life of discipleship is made explicit in the final occurrence of the term in Mark 15:41, in which it is applied to the activity of a large group of women who served Jesus in Galilee and followed him to Jerusalem. It seems important to note that the only human agents to whom this key dis-

---

11. France, *Gospel of Mark*, 108; cf. Beavis, *Mark*, 53; Ernst, *Markus*, 68; Gundry, *Mark*, 91; Lane, *Mark*, 77-78; Stein, *Mark*, 94; Witherington, *Women in the Ministry of Jesus*, 68.

12. Boring, *Mark*, 66; cf. Schnabel, *Mark*, 59.

13. So Theissen, *Miracle Stories*, 66; cf. Miller, *Women in Mark's Gospel*, 22.

14. See, e.g., Black, *Mark*, 75-76; Boring, *Mark*, 66; Donahue and Harrington, *Gospel of Mark*, 85; Edwards, *Mark*, 60; Marcus, *Mark*, 1:199-200; Miller, *Women in Mark's Gospel*, 22-25; Schottroff, *Let the Oppressed Go Free*, 177-78.

Part Two—Narratives *of* Discipleship

cipleship term is attributed, apart from Jesus, are women—those who follow Jesus in the climatic events of the Gospel (Mark 15:40–41, 47; 16:1–8) and Simon's mother-in-law who features in the early stages of the narrative (Mark 1:29–31).

Although some scholars are nervous about developing this linguistic connection in light of the textual distance between Mark 1:31 and 15:41,[15] it may be helpful to note that Mark often uses parallel scenes to frame sections of his Gospel. The clearest example of this occurs in the dual narratives about the healing of blind men in Mark 8:22–26 and 10:46–52. These two stories encompass the major section of Jesus's teaching on the nature of his ministry and discipleship.[16] Mark's passion narrative is likewise framed by two portrayals of anointing, the first by the unnamed but remembered woman (Mark 14:3–9) and the second by the named women at the tomb (Mark 16:1).[17] Given those structural parallels, it seems likely that the two instances of women serving Jesus in Mark 1:31 and 15:41 function as a type of structural frame within which the wider narrative of the Gospel sits. The service of Simon's mother-in-law foreshadows Mark's later assertion that women had in fact been serving Jesus throughout his ministry. And the importance of their activity is conditioned by Jesus's own embodiment of service, especially that manifest in the cross.

The thrust of the structural argument, then, is this: one of the foundational marks of Jesus's ministry is service, and the women mentioned in Mark 1 and 15 serve as narrative embodiments of that aspect of discipleship. This argument, however, is not meant to suggest that the domestic context of Mark 1:29–31 should be left behind. In contrast, the later uses of the term "service" function to heighten the impact of the domestic setting in Mark 1. I am in agreement with Richard Bauckham that while the terminology of service does not always refer specifically to domestic activity, it never loses its reference to the type of work that women and slaves were frequently

---

15. See, e.g., Gundry, *Mark*, 91. See also Krause, "Simon Peter's Mother-in-Law," 37–53. Krause argues against what she sees as a trend in feminist interpretations of Mark's Gospel to redeem Simon's mother-in-law. Krause is right to argue that interpreters should not attempt to spin the narrative positively simply because of gender. It seems, however, that Krause overlooks the narrative function of both Mark's terminology and his use of minor characters as exemplars. This particular narrative cannot bear the weight of the entire scope of Markan discipleship, but neither should it be discarded due either to its narrative position or its brevity.

16. See esp. Marcus, *Mark*, 2:589; cf. Collins, *Mark*, 397; Moloney, *Gospel of Mark*, 163.

17. Cf. Malbon, "Minor Characters," 77.

Restored Discipleship (Mark 1 and 5)

called on to accomplish in the first century CE.[18] Jesus's declaration that his ministry is defined by service does not remove the potential social stigma from the activity, thereby elevating it to a new place of prominence in the community. It is just the opposite. Jesus redefines the importance of status in terms of the context of service. The humility and position reflected in the activity of the domestic service of women and slaves becomes the paradigm for Christian activity.[19] In the present context, it is Simon's mother-in-law who demonstrates this aspect of Christian discipleship in response to her physical restoration.

Mark's brief note about this woman's response to Jesus's act of restoration represents an initial narrative embodiment of the service-oriented nature of Markan discipleship. Her service is not simply a return to standard cultural practice. It is a narrative expression of her commitment to the way that Jesus will himself embody. Her service is not simply repayment for Jesus's act of restoration. It is an embodied reflection of the same service that she has experienced. To lean again on the insightful study of Miller, the "woman's response of service illustrates the reciprocity of the gospel, since her healing enables her to serve her community."[20] With this short narrative in the opening section of the Gospel Mark begins to develop the shape of faithful discipleship that will emerge in the rest of the narrative. The arrival of the kingdom that Jesus embodies in his incarnation is already having restorative impact upon those whom he encounters. The narrative of Simon's mother-in-law offers us an initial portrait of the reality and shape of restored discipleship.

THE BLEEDING WOMAN (MARK 5:25–34)

The narrative of the bleeding woman functions as the central section of a Markan intercalation—a "literary sandwich" in which one story is inserted into another to create a mutually interpretive framework.[21] In the present context, the healing of this woman is inserted into the middle of the dramatic narrative about Jairus and his daughter. The significant number of connections (and contrasts) that exist between the two stories estab-

18. Bauckham, *Gospel Women*, 164. See also Clarke, *Pauline Theology*, 60–71.
19. See the incisive comments in Schottroff, *Let the Oppressed Go Free*, 177–78.
20. Miller, *Women in Mark's Gospel*, 24.
21. On Mark's use of this literary technique, see Shepherd, "Markan Intercalation," 522–40.

Part Two—Narratives of Discipleship

lishes their interconnected function. Each story provides the interpretive context in which the significance of the other develops. Furthermore, the contextual relationship between these two stories is important for understanding the narrative implications that each has for the wider movement of Mark's Gospel. Their narrative connection draws out a number of important points about the nature of Markan Christology and Mark's portrayal of discipleship.

Without intending to detract from the contextual association between the two narratives, the aim of the present section is to focus more specifically on the healing of the bleeding woman and its implications for Mark's paradigm of restored discipleship. In spite of the clear connections between this woman and Jairus's daughter—both of whom are beneficiaries of Jesus's restorative power—the bleeding woman takes a more central role in the narrative. She is not only a narrative foil for Jairus's daughter, but also for Jairus himself. In addition, Candida Moss argues that the woman is also a foil for Jesus. To use Moss's somewhat provocative language, both Jesus and the bleeding woman have "porous" or "leaky" bodies, and their intersection forms a central component of the theological emphasis of the woman's story.[22] In contrast to the narrative of Jairus's daughter, whose experience provides an essential portrait of restoration and a precursor to Jesus's own resurrection, Mark's narrative of the bleeding woman provides a more developed portrait of both her situation and her interaction with Jesus. Her narrative demonstrates not only restoration but also restored discipleship.

Restored Life

The introduction of the woman in Mark 5:25–26 consists of an extended description of her acute medical situation. She suffers from what Mark refers to as a "flow of blood" (ῥύσει αἵματος)—most likely a reference to a form of severe vaginal bleeding outside the boundaries of normal menstruation—which defined her existence for twelve years.[23] In an attempt to resolve the pain and suffering of her condition the woman sought medical treatment from a number of physicians, spending a significant amount of her monetary resources in an attempt to regain her health. Neither the physicians nor their treatment provided her with any reprieve. In fact, Mark informs us that the woman's condition worsened under their care. It is this

22. Moss, "Man with the Flow of Power," 507–19.
23. On the nature of the woman's bleeding, see Collins, *Mark*, 280.

Restored Discipleship (Mark 1 and 5)

severe reality of the woman's medical condition that provides the narrative background for her subsequent action. Having heard about Jesus's ministry, she approaches him from behind in the midst of the crowd, seeking to gain her health through physical contact with Jesus's clothing. The result of her action is instantaneous. The immediacy of her healing creates a clear contrast between the failure of the many physicians who had treated her and Jesus who provides healing without even being initially aware of the event.[24] The pervasive reality of her suffering is overturned in an outpouring of restorative power from Jesus's body.

While the subsequent dialogue between the woman and Jesus highlights the importance of her faith in the restorative process, Mark's initial narration of the story revolves primarily around the event of the restoration itself. The complex introduction of the woman in Mark 5:25–26 is replaced with a concise assertion of her restored condition in Mark 5:29. The stark nature of the contrast is one of the primary ways in which the woman's narrative intersects with that of Jairus's daughter. The severe nature of her medical condition and the immediacy of her restoration provide a narrative parallel to the extraordinary transition from death to life in Mark 5:35–43. In my estimation, the primary theological point of both narratives is that Jesus embodies the restorative power of the new creation inherent in God's kingdom.[25] The dramatic restoration of these two women from conditions of severe medical despair and death evokes the present reality and implications of this in-breaking kingdom. This is not to suggest that Mark's christological emphasis overshadows the narrative of either woman. In contrast, it is precisely in the interaction of Jesus and the women that Mark's wider points about Christology and the life of discipleship emerge. The two realities are necessarily related. In particular, the interaction between Jesus and the bleeding woman echoes the theme of restoration developed in the healing of Simon's mother-in-law, and serves as an additional example of the nature of restored discipleship. The bleeding woman's narrative demonstrates an aspect of Mark's Christology and widens the portrait of discipleship that develops in the Gospel.

Both the portrait of the woman that Mark develops and her own covert interaction with Jesus are frequently read in light of an assumed

---

24. Cf. Bayer, *Markus*, 231; Haber, "A Woman's Touch," 182; Moss, "Man with the Flow of Power," 508 n. 2.

25. So too Miller, *Women in Mark's Gospel*, 58: "Mark's presentation of the healing . . . suggests that the power of Jesus to heal is God's power of the new age."

Part Two—Narratives *of* Discipleship

background of cultic purity. More specifically, interpreters often see an implied connection between the present narrative and the sections of the Levitical code that revolve around the uncleanliness of both normal and abnormal menstruation (e.g., Lev 12:7; 15:19–33; 20:18).[26] From this background it is often argued that given the likelihood that the woman's condition represents a chronic abnormality, she would have been in a perpetual state of ceremonial impurity and potentially subject to quarantine (cf. 11QT^a 45:7–17; 46:16–18; 48:14–17; Josephus, *Ant.* 3.261; *m. Nid.* 7:4).[27] The cultic background developed in light of the linguistic associations between Leviticus and Mark's Gospel is then used to describe certain elements of the woman's portrait. In particular, both her apparent need for secrecy in approaching Jesus and her subsequent fear once Jesus attempts to discover the identity of the person who extracted his power are seen to be by-products of the stigma associated with her condition. In other words, some argue that the woman is forced to approach Jesus under the cover of the crowd because of the negative cultural and social implications of her physical uncleanliness, and that she is marked by fear after the healing due to the possibility that her contact with Jesus resulted in him becoming unclean as well.[28] Perhaps the most sustained interpretation along these lines is that of Marla Selvidge, who argues that the woman's narrative is a direct response to the androcentric viewpoint of physical and social suffering created by the regulations in Leviticus.[29] In Selvidge's view, the woman's restoration demonstrates Jesus's rejection of the Levitical constraints that had contributed to her suffering. The removal of the woman's cultic impurity becomes the central focus of the narrative.

There are a number of potential problems, however, with a sustained emphasis on the Levitical purity regulations as the primary fulcrum upon which the woman's narrative pivots. One of the strongest advocates against this particular reading is Shaye Cohen, who argues that there is no evidence in Second Temple Judaism for the systematic isolation of women experiencing either their normal menstruation cycle or abnormal menstrual bleeding, but that this was a later development of rabbinic Judaism in the

---

26. See, e.g., Bayer, *Markus*, 230; France, *Gospel of Mark*, 236–38; Guelich, *Mark 1–8:26*, 296–300; Marcus, *Mark*, 1:357–58; Miller, *Women in Mark's Gospel*, 52–72.

27. So Marcus, *Mark*, 1:357.

28. See, e.g., Marshall, *Faith*, 106.

29. See Selvidge, "Mark 5:25–34 and Leviticus 15:19–20," 619–23; cf. Dewey, "Jesus' Healings of Women," 126–27.

Restored Discipleship (Mark 1 and 5)

sixth or seventh century CE.[30] Joel Marcus, however, argues that Cohen reads the textual evidence selectively, and that the "surreptitiousness of the woman's approach to Jesus . . . is probably an indirect indication that she is ritually unclean."[31] At the very least, there is some uncertainty about the way in which particular aspects of the Levitical code were practiced in the first century CE.[32] There is also ambiguity about whether the geographical location of the narrative may impact this discussion. Given the strong connection between Leviticus and the temple cult, it is unclear, even if the Levitical regulations concerning menstruation were practiced in the first century CE, whether they would have impacted life in Galilee or only in Jerusalem where the temple was of central importance.[33]

In light of Mark's extended description of the woman's medical condition it seems quite likely that her impurity does function as part of the contextual background of the narrative. Her healing parallels Jesus's preceding interaction with the Gerasene demoniac who was isolated from the community but approaches Jesus when he sees him from a distance (Mark 5:1–20). Mark's initial portrayal of the woman suggests that her approach toward Jesus stands against her cultural and social isolation. While Marcus and others are correct that the cultural context of the narrative implies the unclean status of the woman, it is important to note that this is not an aspect of the woman's story that Mark stresses.[34] The primary focus of the narrative is on the gravity of the woman's medical condition and the dramatic nature of the immediate healing she receives. Even if Marcus is correct that Cohen has misread the evidence about the way in which the regulations of Leviticus were applied in this era of Judaism, Cohen is still right to assert that the narrative itself "does not give any indication that the woman was impure or suffered any degree of isolation as a result of her affliction."[35] A more balanced approach is developed in the constructive contribution of Susan Haber, who argues that Mark's explicit emphasis is

---

30. Cohen, "Menstruants and the Sacred," 273–99; cf. D'Angelo, "Gender and Power in the Gospel of Mark," 83–109; Fonrobert, "The Woman with a Blood-Flow," 121–40.

31. Marcus, *Mark*, 1:357.

32. For a nuanced discussion, see Haber, "A Woman's Touch," 174–80.

33. For contrasting opinions about the influence of geography on purity regulations in the first century CE, see Cohen, "Menstruants and the Sacred," 279; and Haber, "A Woman's Touch," 177–80.

34. So also Haber, "A Woman's Touch," 171–92; and Stein, *Mark*, 267–69.

35. Cohen, "Menstruants and the Sacred," 279.

Part Two — Narratives *of* Discipleship

the woman's health.³⁶ Her impurity is a cultural and contextual reality, but it is not the explicit focus of the narrative.

In contrast to other sections of Mark's Gospel that revolve specifically around cultic regulations (e.g., Mark 2:13–17; 7:1–23), there is no narrated objection to Jesus's interaction with the woman in the present context.³⁷ The disciples are incredulous with Jesus due to the size of the crowd, not due to the reality of the woman's status. Likewise, in the subsequent scene, those gathered at Jairus's house do not appear to be concerned with purity regulations. Their objection revolves not around the potential for Jesus to become unclean by coming into contact with a corpse, but with the notion that he could heal one. There is also a distinction between the present narrative and that of Jesus's healing of the leper (Mark 1:40–44). At that stage of the Gospel, Mark explicitly narrates the subsequent need for the man to demonstrate his cleanliness before the priest. This explicit cultic emphasis appears neither in the narrative of the bleeding woman nor that of Jairus's daughter, despite the background of impurity present in both scenes. The thread that runs through these interconnected narratives in Mark 5 is not that Jesus overrides particular cultic regulations, but that he embodies the life-giving power of God's kingdom.

That there is a particular emphasis in the narrative on the concept of life arises again in the connection between the woman's story and that of Jairus's daughter. Mark's provision of the additional information that the girl was twelve years old (Mark 5:42) suggests that she was of marriageable age at the time of her death. Her revivification is not only a return to life but also a return of her potential to be life-bearing. Similarly, the chronic gynecological problem that plagued the woman for twelve years would have prevented her from being a source of life. In the words of Francis Moloney:

> The young woman, who now begins to pour forth her life in menstruation, and the older woman, who experiences menstruation as a pathological condition, are both restored. They are "given" new life. Here we find that the life-giving powers of women, manifested in the flow of blood, are not "bad" or "impure" (the older woman). Nor are they the cause of problems for Jesus as he touches the younger woman. They are not to be cut off in death (the younger woman). They are "restored" so that the women can go and live in

---

36. Haber, "A Woman's Touch," 171–92; cf. Betsworth, *Reign of God*, 3–5.
37. Cf. D'Angelo, "(Re)Presentations of Women in the Gospels," 141.

Restored Discipleship (Mark 1 and 5)

shalom . . . in the well-being of God's reigning presence, which has "touched" their lives in Jesus of Nazareth.[38]

The primary connection between the two women is their restored life. Jesus's restorative power overrides both medical despair and death, returning the women to a state of wholeness that is evocative of the reality of God's kingdom.[39] Although the cultural background of both narratives likely suggests the presence of cultic impurity, Mark's emphasis lies on the dramatic extent of the restoration of these women in light of the extraordinary crisis which each faces. As with Simon's mother-in-law, they are restored to the fullness of life.

Restored Faith

The narrative of the bleeding woman is defined not only by the reality of her restoration but also its implications. In Mark's continued portrait of positive interactions with Jesus, this woman's narrative functions as a further statement about the nature of discipleship. The primary characteristic that defines Mark's portrayal is that of faith. Jesus's final statement to the woman consists of a commendation of this characteristic. It is her faith— her trust or allegiance—that has saved her (ἡ πίστις σου σέσωκέν σε; Mark 5:34). This is not merely Mark's method for reinserting a theological concept back into a narrative which to this stage has focused primarily on the agency of the woman. It is, rather, confirmation that the entire narrative is a description of the woman's faithful action. The primary import of the interaction between her and Jesus is a demonstration of allegiance (πίστις) to the restorative power of the kingdom embodied in Jesus's ministry.

Given the frequent argument that the primary contextual background revolves around the cultic uncleanliness brought about by the woman's medical condition, the fact that she approaches Jesus from behind in the midst of the crowd (ἐλθοῦσα ἐν τῷ ὄχλῳ ὄπισθεν) is often seen as the result

---

38. Moloney, *Gospel of Mark*, 111. Moloney's argument loudly echoes the similar sentiment put forth by Schüssler Fiorenza, *In Memory of Her*, 124: "The young woman who begins to menstruate, like the older woman who experiences menstruation as a pathological condition, are both 'given' new life. The life-creating powers of women manifested in 'the flow of blood' are neither 'bad' nor cut off in death but are 'restored' so that women can 'go and live in *shalom*,' in the eschatological well-being and happiness of God." See also Donahue and Harrington, *Gospel of Mark*, 281; Haber, "A Woman's Touch," 188–89.

39. Cf. Schüssler Fiorenza, *In Memory of Her*, 122–24.

Part Two — Narratives *of* Discipleship

of her covert intention to avoid direct engagement with Jesus (Mark 5:27). In spite of this assumption, Mark does not provide any explicit explanation for the reason that the woman approaches Jesus in this way. Her presence *within* the crowd, however, may suggest again that the emphasis of the narrative does not revolve around purity regulations. In light of the chronic nature of her condition it seems unlikely that her social status would have been unknown in the community. Moreover, if one assumes that the woman acts secretly due to the fear that she may contaminate Jesus, it is unclear why she would not have had similar empathy for other people in the crowd with whom she would have come in contact. Mark's introductory comment that the surrounding crowd was large (Mark 5:24) and the disciples' later amazement at Jesus's question in light of the crowd's size (Mark 5:31), both suggest that the woman would have been in contact with a large number of people. These contextual realities seem to point again to the notion that Mark's emphasis rests not on the cultic status of the woman but upon the severity of her physical condition.

Likewise, Mark's narration of the woman's internal monologue depicts not a form of timidity or secrecy but an expression of certainty. The woman believes that even if she comes into contact with Jesus's clothing she will be healed. The notion that healing could be extracted even from an individual's garments is often understood to be part of the religious milieu of the first century CE.[40] The later note in Mark 6:56 that wherever Jesus went people similarly sought to gain healing by coming into contact with his clothing suggests that the woman's present desire is neither unusual nor inappropriate (cf. Mark 3:10). Her action is not one of deception but a result of her desperation. In his extensive analysis of the theme of faith in Mark's Gospel, Christopher Marshall helpfully explains that even if it is possible to see magical connotations in the woman's desire to touch Jesus's clothing, her action itself does not reflect superstition. It is an act of genuine faith.[41] As Marshall argues, the "woman's confidence centres on the person of Jesus . . . and the expression 'even his garments' marks the intensity of her conviction."[42] The woman's action is defined by a form of trust or allegiance marked by the certainty of her belief.

As with the narrative of the Syrophoenician woman (Mark 7:24–30), one of the dramatic elements of the present narrative is that of the woman's

---

40. Collins, *Mark* 281–82; cf. Aune, "Magic in Early Christianity," 1507–57.
41. Marshall, *Faith*, 104–6.
42. Ibid., 106; cf. Hurtado, *Mark*, 87.

Restored Discipleship (Mark 1 and 5)

initiative. An array of human physicians has failed to offer her physical reprieve, but her recognition of the efficacy of Jesus's restorative power leads her to initiate contact with him. The narrative emphasis is upon neither secrecy nor superstition but rather upon the woman's agency in the midst of her severe situation. She extracts power from Jesus without his prior consent. The woman approaches Jesus in the belief that she will be healed, and she is.[43] Malbon's use of the terms "bold," "faithful," and "active" in conjunction with the woman are accurate descriptions of this instance of Markan characterization.[44] The woman's initiative is not something that is overturned by Jesus later in the narrative. His declaration of healing in Mark 5:34 is a public confirmation of what the woman knew immediately in her own body—that the restorative power of Jesus had brought her back to life.

In contrast to this positive assessment, the woman's response to her immediate restoration is often seen to be an indictment against her. That Mark describes the woman as conditioned by "fear and trembling" (φοβηθεῖσα καὶ τρέμουσα; Mark 5:33) is put forth as evidence that she is not a completely positive character. Marshall, for example, argues that the woman's "fear at Jesus' reaction to her deed represents a defect in her understanding of his character which must yet be remedied."[45] The woman's fear is also sometimes associated with the narrative of the twelve disciples in Mark 4 in which their lack of faith during the storm on the sea is closely connected with their fear (Mark 4:37–41).[46] In the context of Mark 4, the disciples wake Jesus and question his concern for them in the midst of the storm. Jesus responds by rebuking them, questioning their lack of faith. The specific note of the disciples' fear in Mark 4:41 (ἐφοβήθησαν φόβον μέγαν), however, does not relate back to Jesus's rebuke but is rather a description of the disciples' response to Jesus's ability to calm the storm.[47] In the immediate context of Mark 4 the disciples' fear is not an example of their failure but a description of their response to a divine disclosure. It is this aspect of the disciples' narrative that is paralleled in the woman's experience. Mark

---

43. Cf. Stein, *Mark*, 268.
44. Malbon, "Fallible Followers," 36–37.
45. Marshall, *Faith*, 106; cf. Tolbert, *Sowing the Gospel*, 169.
46. See, e.g., Beavis, "Women as Models of Faith," 6; Williams, *Other Followers*, 115–16.
47. So Bauckham, *Gospel Women*, 290; cf. Collins, *Mark*, 800; Dwyer, *Motif of Wonder*, 109–11; Marcus, *Mark*, 1:334.

Part Two—Narratives *of* Discipleship

does not describe her fear either as something that is overcome before she approaches Jesus or as the way in which she approaches him. It is rather a description of her reaction given her knowledge of what has taken place.[48] At the risk of overstatement, we might say that her physical restoration represents an internal theophany—she comes into contact with the divine and responds accordingly with fear and trembling (cf. Mark 5:15; 16:5-8).

That the woman's fear is not an obstacle that needed to be overcome in Mark's development of the narrative is supported by Jesus's statement to the woman: "'Daughter, your faith has saved you. Go in peace and live a life restored from your affliction'" (Mark 5:34). Jesus's words function neither as a reassessment of the event nor as its completion. In contrast, they reflect a public confirmation of what had already been accomplished. Jesus commends the trust or faith that the woman exhibits by her action and encourages her to pursue an existence marked by the reality of her restoration. The unique dimension of Jesus's statement is that he frames her activity as the agent which creates her restored condition. Removed from its narrative context, Jesus's statement about the woman's faith may seem to imply that it is possible for restoration to emerge solely through human agency. The woman produces her own healing and salvation. There is certainly a narrative emphasis on the woman's initiative and agency. She parallels both the Gerasene demoniac (Mark 5:1-20) and Jairus (Mark 5:21-24, 35-43) in approaching Jesus without any prior engagement on his part. But in all three instances the human initiative is directed at a specific object, namely Jesus himself. To lean again on the work of Marshall, it is helpful to note that "the woman's entire orientation is toward Jesus as the one through whom such salvation is available. . . . The woman's faith has saved her because it has permitted the 'going forth power' of Jesus to do its intended work in her life."[49] The woman's extraction of power out of Jesus's body constitutes both a manifestation of divine agency and a demonstration of her own faithfulness.

Restored Identity

Jesus's personal engagement with the woman also reflects a significant transition in Mark's narrative. She is no longer defined in reference to her

---

48. Cf. Guelich, *Mark*, 298; Hooker, *Mark*, 149; Moloney, *Gospel of Mark*, 108; Strauss, *Mark*, 231.

49. Marshall, *Faith*, 108.

Restored Discipleship (Mark 1 and 5)

chronic bleeding. She is a daughter—a member of the community.[50] Jesus's words evoke the reality of her restored identity. In her study on daughters in Mark's Gospel, Sharon Betsworth notes that Jesus's reference to the woman as daughter highlights both his affection for her and her position within the new family defined by the kingdom established in and through his ministry.[51] In Mark 3:31–35 Jesus offers an important reassessment of the nature of family. Within God's kingdom family is no longer defined in terms of biology but rather in terms of association with Jesus himself. As Boring notes, "the one who is the Son of God here declares that those about him are not only followers and disciples, and not only brothers and sisters to each other, but that as their brother they belong *with* him as brothers and sisters to the family of God."[52] This woman's initiative in trusting Jesus identifies her not as someone excluded from the community but as a representative of its reality. Her experience is a narrative embodiment of the existence of the new family established in the inauguration of God's kingdom. Indeed, within the present context, the woman becomes the key exemplar for Jairus, portraying the need for trust in the restorative power of God's kingdom in the midst of severe circumstances. Her narrative is a portrait of restored discipleship.

CONCLUSION

The purpose of this chapter was to describe the way in which the narratives of Simon's mother-in-law (Mark 1:29–31) and the bleeding woman (Mark 5:25–34) function within Mark's wider portrayal of narrative discipleship. I argued that Jesus's interaction with these two women creates a portrait of *restored discipleship*. Each woman encounters Jesus in the midst of a medical crisis and is impacted by the restorative power of God's kingdom. Their restoration is not merely a description of their physical restoration, but the inauguration of a life defined by the kingdom. The story of each woman functions as a narrative embodiment of characteristics of discipleship that Mark highlights throughout the progression of the Gospel. Simon's mother-in-law embodies the essential characteristic of service, while the significant transition of the bleeding woman from death to life evokes the essential characteristic of faith. This mother and daughter are drawn into the new

50. Haber, "A Woman's Touch," 184.
51. Betsworth, *Reign of God*, 103–7; cf. Miller, *Women in Mark's Gospel*, 60.
52. Boring, *Mark*, 110 (original emphasis).

Part Two — Narratives *of* Discipleship

family created in and through Jesus's ministry. They are restored disciples and exemplars of restored discipleship.

4

Spoken Discipleship (Mark 7)

INTRODUCTION

GOD'S KINGDOM IS TRANSFORMATIVE. Mark's narrative relates the particular ways in which the kingdom—both spoken by and embodied in Jesus—re-creates and restores the world. The spoken message of Jesus is central to Mark's development of this transformative narrative of the kingdom. It is this spoken message that brings about a reordering of the human story. Mark's narrative begins with an emphasis on Jesus's declaration of the good news of God's in-breaking kingdom (Mark 1:14–15), Jesus's desire to proclaim the message widely (Mark 1:38), and the appointment of disciples to participate in this same act of proclamation (Mark 3:14). One of the central trajectories in Mark's Gospel is the extension of this act of proclamation from Jesus to the disciples. To become a participant in the narrative of the kingdom requires learning to speak the language of the kingdom.

The foundational grammar of the kingdom is God's act of restoration. The reality of divine restoration that Mark illustrates in the narratives of Simon's mother-in-law (Mark 1:29–31) and the bleeding woman (Mark 5:25–34) impacts the progression of the Gospel. The question that emerges from their stories is how one is meant to embody this narrative of restoration in life and action? One of the key ways in which Mark answers this question is through his intentional portrayal of subsequent women in the narrative. The traits which they display in their individual narratives

Part Two—Narratives *of* Discipleship

offer a holistic paradigm of essential characteristics of what it means to be a follower of Jesus. Within these narratives we can see that the restored life brought about by God's in-breaking kingdom creates disciples that speak the language of the kingdom, embody the sacrificial action that it demands, and conform their lives around the shape of the cross.

My intention in the present chapter is to examine how the narrative of the Syrophoenician woman (Mark 7:24–30) helps us to understand the first of these aspects of discipleship—the call to speak the language of God's kingdom. As with the preceding chapter, my central aim is to describe the way in which the Syrophoenician woman serves as a narrative example of Markan discipleship. I want to suggest that her narrative displays a key focus on speech. Mark's portrait of the Syrophoenician woman is a narrative of *spoken discipleship*. Our attention will focus on the woman's culturally audacious exchange with Jesus. Her persistent interaction with Jesus despite the presence of explicit ethnic, geographic, and gender-related divides creates a portrait of discipleship that exists irrespective of those boundaries and embodies a distinct aspect of God's kingdom.

THE SYROPHOENICIAN WOMAN (MARK 7:24–30)

The narrative of the Syrophoenician woman begins with Jesus crossing into the Gentile region of Tyre—a city about sixty kilometers northwest of Galilee—on his own initiative. Mark does not immediately outline a specific reason for the journey and so its intended result is somewhat enigmatic. Jesus is apparently seeking privacy as he enters into an unidentified house in the region where he hopes to remain anonymous. As in both Mark 2:1 and 3:20 where news of Jesus's entrance into a house results in the gathering of a crowd, his present desire for anonymity here goes unmet. Even in this non-Jewish region his presence cannot be kept secret and an individual woman from the area quickly comes to request healing for her demon-possessed daughter. Perhaps unexpectedly, her plea is met with an initial rejection from Jesus—"Permit the children to be satisfied first, for it is not right to take the bread from the children and throw it to the dogs" (Mark 7:27). In spite of Jesus's initial rejection of her request, the woman continues to engage with him, suggesting that there is enough food for both the "children" and the "dogs" to receive their required portions. In light of her response, Jesus acquiesces to her plea and the woman returns home to find her daughter restored to health.

Spoken Discipleship (Mark 7)

Although the progression of the narrative is relatively straightforward, the harsh nature of the exchange between Jesus and the woman is confronting. Given Jesus's earlier positive engagement with Simon's mother-in-law (Mark 1:29–31), the woman with persistent bleeding (Mark 5:25–34), and Jairus's daughter (Mark 5:21–24, 35–43), his initial refusal of this woman's request seems out of place. Although Jesus eventually provides healing for the woman's daughter, questions remain concerning the stark nature of their encounter. Interpreters of Mark's Gospel often attempt to explain both the overtly harsh nature of Jesus's engagement with the woman and her intriguing response. Because of the controversial and enigmatic nature of their dialogue, the overarching theological impact of the woman's narrative is often left behind in favor of a focus upon its constituent parts, with efforts either to rescue Jesus from the negative impact of his statement or to praise the woman for her extraordinary persistence and wit. Both of these aspects of the narrative are essential in helping us to illuminate its broader function in Mark's narrative. There is an exegetical risk, however, in focusing so intently on the scene's dialogical trees that we lose sight of the narrative forest. The import of the narrative is dependent not only on the sum of its parts but also on its place within the larger context of the Gospel.[1]

We are interested here both in the specific details of the narrative and the way in which the narrative—especially its key participants—functions more widely in Mark's Gospel. More specifically, we want to attend to the question of how Mark's presentation of the Syrophoenician woman contributes to his wider portrayal of discipleship. As a way to emphasize the *dramatic* nature of the narrative the following analysis will be structured around theatrical terms. We will consider the stage upon which the narrative takes place, the script that encompasses the dialogical engagement between the woman and Jesus, and the way in which the Syrophoenician woman performs the message of the gospel.

Setting the Stage—Contextual and Narrative Backgrounds

Once the woman comes to Jesus with her request, their subsequent dialogue becomes the central focus and the geographic position of the narrative is often left in the contextual background. It would be a mistake, however, to diminish the geographical and cultural setting of what follows. Gerd Theissen's influential socio-historical analysis of the Gospels has

1. Cf. France, *Gospel of Mark*, 296.

Part Two—Narratives *of* Discipleship

helped interpreters of Mark's Gospel to grasp the reality that the socio-economic and political relationship between Tyre and Galilee was significantly strained.[2] The agricultural relationship between the two areas was often particularly tenuous, with the result that there was a sharp economic divide between urban Tyre and rural Galilee.[3] The Jewish historian Josephus notes that the political relationship between the two areas was also acrimonious due to past injustices related to both economic disparity and geographical expansion (*Ant.* 14.313–321). Some aspects of this tension came to fruition in the circumstances surrounding the Jewish War (66–73 CE), during which the Tyrians killed and imprisoned a significant number of Jews (*J.W.* 2.478).[4] The economic and political divisions that existed between the two geographic areas were severe enough for Josephus to refer to the residents of Tyre as hostile enemies to the Jews (*Ag. Ap.* 1.71).[5] Given this information, Mark's specific identification of the location of the narrative provides a dramatic backdrop to the subsequent dialogue. Jesus's abusive distinction between the children and the dogs with respect to the appropriate distribution of bread may stem at least in part from the inherent socio-economic and political tension that plagued the region.[6]

That the geographic context is crucial to the narrative is confirmed by the dual identification of the woman when she is introduced in Mark 7:26. Mark describes the woman in terms of both her cultural—"Greek" (Ἑλληνίς)—and national—"Syrophoenician by birth" (Συροφοινίκισσα τῷ γένει)—identities. Although the initial description of the woman as a "Greek" may simply signify that she is a Gentile (cf. Rom 1:16; 1 Cor 1:22–24), it may also point to a more nuanced understanding of her background in terms of language, cultural integration, and socio-economic and political status. In light of the cultural progress of Hellenization and later novel interpretations of the Syrophoenician woman's biography (e.g., Ps.-Clem. *Hom.* 13.7), Theissen argues that this description suggests that the woman belonged to a relatively high social class.[7]

---

2. Theissen, *Gospels in Context*, 61–80. On the importance of geographical locations in Mark's narrative, see Malbon, *Narrative Space*.

3. Theissen, *Gospels in Context*, 72–75.

4. Cf. Marcus, *Mark*, 1:471; Theissen, *Gospels in Context*, 75–77.

5. Cf. Marcus, *Mark*, 1:462; Schnabel, *Mark*, 172; Theissen, *Gospels in Context*, 77; Witherington, *Women in the Ministry of Jesus*, 168.

6. Marcus, *Mark*, 1:462.

7. Theissen, *Gospels in Context*, 68–72; cf. Bengston, "Syrien in der hellenistischen Zeit," 252; Donahue and Harrington, *Gospel of Mark*, 223.

Spoken Discipleship (Mark 7)

In addition, that the woman is a "Syrophoenician by birth" highlights her regional affiliation and confirms her relation to the hostile area in which the narrative unfolds. This dual description of the woman brings the geographical setting of the story into focus and highlights the dramatic ethnic distinction between the woman and Jesus.[8] Whereas Mark's audience may have been initially predisposed to empathize with Simon's mother-in-law (Mark 1:29–31) and the woman with persistent bleeding (Mark 5:25–34) given their dire physical situations, the nuanced identification of the Syrophoenician woman positions her as a community outsider. Both the geographical setting of the narrative and the geopolitical identification of the woman frame the subsequent dialogue. Given the significant ethnic and geographic boundaries that stand between Jesus and the woman, it may actually be the positive conclusion to their interaction—not Jesus's initial refusal of her request—that constitutes the most unexpected aspect of the narrative.

Although she may not be a contextually sympathetic character, Mark's introduction of this Greek Syrophoenician woman does have significant parallels with the narrative of the bleeding woman (Mark 5:25–34). Beyond their basic connection in terms of gender, their narratives are coordinated in several more substantial ways. Mark's description of the Syrophoenician woman hearing about Jesus and falling at his feet (Mark 7:25) echoes his earlier introduction of the bleeding woman (Mark 5:27, 33).[9] And, despite the drastic circumstances surrounding each woman, their interaction with Jesus is marked by persistence. The unnamed woman in Mark 5 endures a remarkable amount of physical suffering prior to approaching Jesus, while the Syrophoenician woman moves past the immense cultural divide that separated both herself and her daughter from Jesus. This parallel development of persistence leads Elizabeth Struthers Malbon to assert that both women are characterized by the "active faith" that is a defining characteristic for disciples in Mark's Gospel (e.g., Mark 2:1–5; 5:24–29, 35–36; 9:14–27; 10:52).[10] In spite of what might be seen as a pejorative contextual introduction, the Syrophoenician woman's narrative evokes key connections with an earlier example of narrative discipleship.

The thematic parallels between the two women, however, also serve to emphasize the stark difference in the way that Jesus initially responds to

---

8. Cf. Miller, *Women in Mark's Gospel*, 91–94.
9. Marcus, *Mark*, 1:466–67; Moloney, *Gospel of Mark*, 145.
10. Malbon, "Fallible Followers," 37; cf. Marshall, *Faith*, 237.

Part Two—Narratives *of* Discipleship

each woman. Although we may have a set of presumed assumptions about how a man would have been expected to respond to a woman in the first century CE, Jesus's positive interaction with the bleeding woman creates a certain amount of contextual dissonance for the audience when Jesus then responds negatively to the Syrophoenician woman's request.[11] This same type of contextual dissonance arises from the relationship between the narratives of the Syrophoenician woman and Jairus (Mark 5:21–24, 35–43). Although these two figures are ostensibly different in terms of their ethnicity, gender, and social position, their narrative situations develop along similar lines. Each approaches Jesus in a position of humility with the hope of receiving healing for a suffering daughter from a source outside of their normal context (Mark 5:22–23; 7:25–26).[12] Jairus's narrative is another contextual foil for the Syrophoenician woman, and the distinction in Jesus's initial response to both individuals underlines the differences between them. The staging of the Syrophoenician woman's situation along the lines of both of these preceding figures highlights the cultural complexity of her situation and stresses her persistent determination to care for her daughter.

Learning the Script—Exchanging Parables

Jesus's stark response to the woman's plea—"Permit the children to be satisfied first, for it is not right to take the bread from the children and throw it to the dogs" (Mark 7:27)—does not directly address her concern. It is rather a *parable* that develops a particular set of metaphors. The statement has nothing to do with literal children, bread, or dogs, but rather highlights the distinction between Jews and Gentiles emphasized by the contextual placement of the narrative.[13] Indeed, the apparent force of the statement is that it is inappropriate for this cultural outsider "to impose on the 'bread' (i.e., blessings of the kingdom) that rightfully belongs to the 'children' of

---

11. Contra Donahue and Harrington, *Gospel of Mark*, 237.

12. Iverson, *Gentiles in the Gospel of Mark*, 47–48; Miller, *Women in Mark's Gospel*, 92–93.

13. Iverson, *Gentiles in the Gospel of Mark*, 45. Although Mark Nanos has helpfully disputed the notion that the reference to dogs should automatically draw attention to a cultural divide between Jews and Gentiles—it arises not from the cultural identity of the woman but from the household matrix of the parable—it seems clear that the parable itself evokes a cultural contrast in light of its contextual placement in Mark's Gospel (see Nanos, "Paul's Reversal," 469–74).

Spoken Discipleship (Mark 7)

Israel."[14] Thus, in spite of initial confusion about why Jesus utters this particular parable, there is little mystery surrounding its contextual referents. Moreover, that Jesus responds to the woman with a parable does not detract from the reality that his statement is a clear rejection of her request. He focuses on the division between children and dogs as a metaphorical way of speaking about the perceived contrast between (cultural) insiders and outsiders.[15] The parable functions as an overtly negative rejection of the woman's request in light of her identity as a Greek Syrophoenician.

As a way to mitigate the harsh reality of Jesus's statement, interpreters of Mark's Gospel have heaped a significant amount of weight on Jesus's use of the adjective "first" (πρῶτον). They suggest that the term represents a particular description of salvation history in which Israel has priority and the Gentiles feature only secondarily. In this way Jesus's statement is seen to reflect the same idea inherent in Paul's assertion in Rom 1:16 that the gospel brings about salvation first to the Jew and then to the Gentile.[16] The import of this argument is that Jesus's response does not constitute a rejection of the woman's request but rather positions it at an appropriate place on the salvation-historical timeline.

Although Mark does use the term "first" in contexts pertaining to historical timelines (e.g., Mark 3:27; 4:28; 9:11–12; 13:10), the difficulty with emphasizing any type of temporal scheme in the present narrative is that the woman's response to Jesus does not suggest that she finds some measure of hope in the possibility of a *later* feeding of the dogs.[17] She understands his parable as a rejection of her request and seeks to create a revised frame-

14. Iverson, *Gentiles in the Gospel of Mark*, 48.

15. The reference to dogs is almost certainly negative in the present context. In the wider New Testament, dogs are associated with both unclean swine (Matt 7:6) and heretics (Phil 3:2; 2 Pet 2:22; Rev 22:15), and the broader biblical tradition uses language about dogs in similarly negative ways (e.g., Exod 22:31; 1 Sam 17:43; 1 Kgs 21:23; 22:38; 2 Kgs 8:13; 9:36; Prov 26:11; Isa 56:10–11). The notion that the diminutive form of κυνάρια somehow makes the statement more palatable, creating a scene involving the interaction with children and "little puppies" in a household, is untenable (contra, e.g., Edwards, *Mark*, 219–20). In the New Testament diminutives frequently reflect no apparent distinction in meaning from their regular forms and the presence of a number of diminutives within the present context (i.e., θυγάτριον; κυνάρια; ψιχίων; παιδίον) is a reminder of the fact that Mark uses these particular forms more frequently than any other New Testament writer (BDF §111). For the notion that the diminutive form itself has negative connotations in the present context, see Cadwallader, *Beyond the Word of a Woman*, 74–81.

16. Cf. Boring, *Mark*, 211–12.

17. Contra Stein, *Mark*, 352.

Part Two—Narratives *of* Discipleship

work in which her daughter can receive the benefits of Jesus's ministry simultaneously—"even the dogs under the table eat the crumbs from the children" (Mark 7:28). Her immediate focus centers on the notion of *exclusivity* not *temporality*.[18] This connects well with the contextual setting that Mark has created for his audience by emphasizing the geographic location of the narrative and the geopolitical identity of the woman. The question the narrative raises is not *when* will these women receive the benefits of the kingdom, but rather *can* they receive them?

The parable which the woman speaks back to Jesus actually seems to be a better description of Jesus's ministry up to this point of the Gospel narrative than his own negative statement. Although Israel has indeed been the primary focus of Jesus's ministry, Gentiles have not been systematically excluded.[19] Jesus has already healed people from Gentile regions (including Tyre) suffering from unclean spirits (Mark 3:7–12) and has traveled into the region of the Gerasenes, healing a man described as having an unclean spirit and being demon-possessed, and instructing him to relate the act of mercy to his own people (Mark 5:1–20). The eventual restoration of the Syrophoenician woman's daughter from her demon possession provides a further example of Jesus's positive interaction with Gentiles and functions as the catalyst for his continued ministry in Gentile areas (Mark 7:31–8:10). If Mark's use of the term "first" carries any salvation-historical significance, it is that the time for the inclusion of Gentiles into the kingdom is already present in Jesus's ministry.

The narrative structure of Mark 6–8 also highlights the inclusion of the Gentiles into Jesus's messianic program. The initial portion of Jesus's statement in Mark 7:27—"Permit the children to be satisfied first"—likely alludes to the broader narrative of the Gospel in which Jesus feeds and satisfies both Jews (Mark 6:30–44) and Gentiles (Mark 8:1–9). Mark's incorporation of these two distinct feeding narratives points to the reality that Jesus's ministry is not limited by ethnic boundaries. Both Jews and Gentiles are satisfied by his miraculous provision of bread (Mark 6:42; 8:8). Apart from the feeding narratives in Mark 6 and 8, bread plays an important role in the material that directly precedes the narrative of the Syrophoenician woman in Mark 7. Questions concerning the disciples' consumption of bread with unclean hands (Mark 7:1–5) result in a stark confrontation between Jesus and the Jewish leaders concerning God's commands and

---

18. Guelich, *Mark*, 387; cf. Marcus, *Mark*, 1:466.
19. See Iverson, *Gentiles in the Gospel of Mark*.

Spoken Discipleship (Mark 7)

human traditions (Mark 7:6–13). In response to this confrontation Jesus instructs both the crowd (Mark 7:14–15) and the disciples (Mark 7:17–23) about the way in which a person is defiled. Jesus's central claim is that the product of one's heart is the only measure by which one is defined as either clean or unclean.[20] The notion that neither food nor people are defiled by external factors paves the way for the narrative introduction of the Syrophoenician woman, who becomes a living portrait of this redefinition of cleanliness.[21]

This narrative analysis forces us to reconsider Jesus's apparent rejection of the woman. If it is the Syrophoenician woman's parable that more readily coordinates with Mark's portrayal of Jesus's ministry, then how do we account for Jesus's harsh statement concerning the children and the dogs? The suggestion that I would like to develop is that Jesus's statement represents a particular form of irony. Given both Jesus's engagement with Gentiles at earlier stages of the Gospel and the parabolic form of Jesus's words in the present narrative, one way to understand the controversial nature of Jesus's statement is to identify it as an ironic representation of the negative preconception about cleanliness seen in Mark 7:1–23. To state it in a different way, Jesus's statement ironically reflects a notion similar to the preceding idea that cleanliness is defined by cultic realities. In the same way that certain foods are designated unclean because of cultic traditions, Jesus's statement insinuates that certain *people* are designated unclean because of cultural distinctions. The Syrophoenician woman's own parable is an appropriate response to this negative preconception because it reassesses the situation along lines that coordinate more readily with Jesus's own response in the preceding narrative (Mark 7:18–23).

To support this reading of the narrative it is important that we understand precisely how the term *irony* operates in the present argument. In his important work on the function of irony in Mark's Gospel, Jerry Camery-Hoggatt argues that Jesus's statement in Mark 7:27 should be defined as a piece of "peirastic irony . . . a form of verbal challenge intended to test the other's response."[22] By this he means that Jesus's initial rejection is meant to challenge the woman to respond to an idea that does not actually represent Jesus's own viewpoint. As a way of enhancing Camery-Hoggatt's thesis it

---

20. Ibid., 51.
21. Cf. Aquino and McLemore, "Markan Characterization of Women," 412; Miller, *Women in Mark's Gospel*, 99; Rhoads, "Jesus and the Syrophoenician Woman," 348, 362.
22. Camery-Hoggatt, *Irony in Mark's Gospel*, 150.

Part Two—Narratives *of* Discipleship

may be helpful to develop the notion of irony with the support of relevance theory, a branch of study within the discipline of linguistics. In this particular framework irony is defined as an event in which a statement or thought is asserted by someone so that they can disassociate or distance themselves from its inherent idea.[23]

For example, if I were say to students in my Greek language class, "learning Greek vocabulary is not important to mastering Koine Greek," they would recognize, given their wider experience of my teaching in the subject, that this was not my actual opinion but an assertion of a viewpoint I do not hold and would want to disassociate myself from. The "silliness" or *irony* of the statement would serve to draw the students' attention to my actual viewpoint—"language without vocabulary is silence." Applying this idea to Mark 7, my suggestion is that Jesus's negative response to the Syrophoenician woman does not represent his own perception of the situation. In contrast, it represents the negative assumption held by the Jewish leaders in the preceding narrative about the distinction between clean and unclean foods from which Jesus intends to distance himself. The Syrophoenician woman recognizes that this statement does not accord with the information that led her to approach Jesus initially, and so she responds with a revised parable that reflects her knowledge of the inclusive nature of Jesus's ministry.

By identifying Jesus's statement as a piece of irony my intention is not to mitigate its confrontational nature but to emphasize it. Mark 7:1–23 illustrates the misconception that ritual practice prevents defilement by eliminating the consumption of unclean foods. As a Gentile outsider the Syrophoenician woman serves as a living representation of these unclean foods. Jesus's initial response to the woman functions as an ironic representation of the same harsh attitude of exclusion implicit in the earlier viewpoint of the Jewish leaders. Jesus's response to the preceding argument concerning unclean foods, however, highlights for Mark's audience that this form of exclusion does not reflect Jesus's own viewpoint. The particular form of irony in the present case is not that Jesus pretends to affirm something that he does not. In contrast, the idea is that his representation of the expected state of affairs actually serves to distance or disassociate himself from that conceptual framework.[24] Consequently, the explicit removal of the categories of clean and unclean in relation to food (Mark 7:17–23) is

23. See esp. Noh, *Metarepresentation*, 94–98.
24. Contra Williams, "Mark 7:27," 347.

Spoken Discipleship (Mark 7)

applied in the present narrative to the relationship between people groups so that the external boundaries that would have defined the woman as an outsider are removed.[25] The Syrophoenician woman's parabolic response to Jesus makes it clear that she understands the negative implications of his statement. Because of that reality, she persists in her plea, reformulating the original parable to create a framework in which she and her daughter are included in the blessings of the kingdom.[26]

The significance of both Jesus's statement and the woman's response is determined in large part by their parabolic form. Earlier in the Gospel, Mark establishes that parables are particularly associated with "outsiders" (τοῖς ἔξω; Mark 4:11). He describes the circumstances of "kingdom-outsiders" in terms of the prophetic narrative of Isaiah (Isa 6:9–10) in which those with hardened hearts remain unchanged because of their lack of perception (Mark 4:11–12). The idea developed in Mark 4 is not that parables are a means to exclude outsiders, but rather that their inability to understand Jesus's parables is evocative of their position with respect to the kingdom.[27] For Mark, the conjunction of belief and disbelief surrounding Jesus echoes the situation represented in Isaiah, in which the prophet's ministry also creates a mixed response (Isa 6:9–13). It is important to note, however, that irony is at play in both Isaiah and Mark's Gospel. That Isaiah is commissioned to callous the hearts of his hearers to prevent repentance is ironic in that it represents the opposite of the prophet's contextual mission to bring the people back to the Lord (Isa 6:13). Mark draws on this irony by establishing that the disparate responses to parables are representative of the hardened hearts of the people (cf. Matt 13:15) despite the fact that this is not the desired outcome of Jesus's parables themselves, which are actually meant to elucidate the nature of the kingdom (Mark 4:26–32).[28] One's ability to understand parables then becomes evidence of the status of his or her heart, forging another contextual link between the Syrophoenician woman's narrative and Mark 7:1–23, in which the internal quality of the heart is positioned as the defining characteristic of cleanliness (Mark 7:18–23).

It is certainly significant then that those expected to be insiders, particularly the twelve disciples, often fail to understand the significance of Jesus's parables (e.g., Mark 4:13; 7:18), while this Gentile woman responds

---

25. Edwards, *Mark*, 218–19.
26. Cf. Williams, *Other Followers*, 120.
27. On the function of ἵνα in Mark 4:12, see esp. Sim, *Marking Thought*, 144–48.
28. Ibid.

Part Two—Narratives *of* Discipleship

to him with a parable that establishes her position as insider with ears to hear (cf. Mark 4:9, 23).²⁹ Indeed, the Syrophoenician woman is the only character in Mark's Gospel to demonstrate an immediate understanding of one of Jesus's parables. Even more, she enters into the world of the parable and responds with her own parable that accurately illustrates the truly inclusive reality of the gospel in which the blessings of the kingdom are available to both Jew and Gentile.³⁰ The Syrophoenician woman not only hears Jesus's parable, she herself "parables" back to him. In this she exhibits not only her intelligence but also her position as a kingdom insider. Her response is one of spoken discipleship.

Performing the Dialogue—Speaking Jesus's Logos

The Syrophoenician woman's parable is a key turning point in the narrative. Jesus responds to her statement by fulfilling her original request—the healing of her daughter (Mark 7:29-30). Jesus's response is intriguing both because it stems directly from the woman's persistence and because of its unique phrasing. Jesus informs the woman that it is "because of this word" (διὰ τοῦτον τὸν λόγον) that she may depart to find her daughter restored to health. Within the Gospel, Mark frequently uses the term "word"—λόγος— to refer to Jesus's activity and message (e.g., Mark 2:2; 4:33; 8:38; 13:31).³¹

---

29. Iverson, *Gentiles in the Gospel of Mark*, 52-53; cf. Alonso, *The Woman Who Changed Jesus*, 294; Miller, *Women in Mark's Gospel*, 98.

30. Edwards, *Mark*, 221-22. The notion that the woman enters into the parabolic framework created by Jesus is not meant to suggest that the woman's description of herself and her daughter as dogs under the table somehow reflects her humility, as if she appropriately accepts a lower or secondary status for both herself and her daughter because of their cultural identity (contra Collins, *Mark*, 367-68; France, *Gospel of Mark*, 299; Iverson, *Gentiles in the Gospel of Mark*, 54; Williams, *Other Followers*, 12). That she represents herself and her daughter as dogs is merely an extension of the parable, not an acceptance of the ethnic distinction highlighted in Jesus's ironic representation. That the dogs receive the children's crumbs in the woman's parable is, likewise, neither an expression of temporal sequence nor of some sort of hierarchy of blessing. The purpose of her parabolic reconstruction is to reflect a situation in which Jews and Gentiles *equally* receive the benefits of the kingdom *now*.

31. Out of the twenty-three occurrences of the noun in Mark's Gospel, twenty-one have their referent in Jesus's own activity or refer broadly to the gospel message. Both of the apparent exceptions (Mark 5:36 and 11:29) may actually revolve around the same general principle. In Mark 5:35 some people from Jairus's house inform him of his daughter's death and encourage him to abandon his endeavor with Jesus. In Mark 5:36 Jesus then rejects their word (τὸν λόγον) and exhorts Jairus to believe. There is an implicit

Spoken Discipleship (Mark 7)

In light of this connection, we can see that Jesus's characterization of the woman's statement as λόγος positions her restructured parable within the context of the gospel message.³² The destruction of boundaries between Jew and Gentile developed in the woman's speech-act helps to create a framework for understanding the nature of God's kingdom and its participants. The definition of kingdom insiders is not marked by geopolitical identity but by a capacity to understand and speak the λόγος of Jesus. The woman's parabolic λόγος reflects the inclusivity of the gospel, and Jesus confirms its reality through the miraculous healing of her daughter, an event that for Mark demonstrates the reality of God's in-breaking kingdom.³³ The woman's statement does not change Jesus's mind concerning the situation, but rather functions in Mark's narrative to disassociate the ministry of the kingdom from the strict exclusivity inherent in Jesus's ironic statement about the children and the dogs (Mark 7:27).

The central theme in the woman's narrative revolves around the identification of who may or may not receive the benefits of the kingdom. That Jesus heals the daughter of this acute outsider reverses the expectation of what defines followers of Jesus. Their relationship to him is measured neither by ethnic nor cultural identity. It is measured by participation in kingdom activity, defined in the present narrative as the woman herself speaking the gospel message—Jesus's λόγος.³⁴ God's kingdom develops not through a defense of geographic or cultural boundaries that maintain certain perceptions of holiness but through an overt expansion across boundaries to all those who participate in the gospel of Jesus Christ which has been at the forefront of Mark's narrative since the outset (Mark 1:1). Expectations concerning the identity of outsiders and insiders are then reversed, as this Greek Syrophoenician woman embodies the message of the gospel in her parable. She *speaks* God's kingdom.

---

distinction in the narrative between the others' λόγος and the λόγος Jesus speaks to Jairus (μόνον πίστευε) and his daughter (ταλιθα κουμ; Mark 5:41), both of which provide clarity about his mission. In Mark 11:27–28 a group of Jewish leaders question the authority of Jesus and he in return asks them to answer "one question" (ἕνα λόγον; Mark 11:29) that will "indicate [whether or not] his opponents have caught something of his gospel" (Cadwallader, *Beyond the Word*, 208). Their inability to answer (Mark 11:31–33) is an implicit rejection of Jesus's λόγος.

32. Cadwallader, *Beyond the Word*, 208–9; Miller, *Women In Mark's Gospel*, 110.

33. Miller, *Women in Mark's Gospel*, 94.

34. See also Miller, "Women Characters," 181.

Part Two—Narratives *of* Discipleship

Once we identify the Syrophoenician woman's spoken embodiment of the kingdom in the narrative, the contrast between the woman and the twelve disciples becomes contextually transparent. In the previous narrative the disciples fail to unravel the significance of Jesus's teaching concerning purity regulations (Mark 7:18; cf. 6:52; 8:14–21), while the woman enters into Jesus's parabolic framework and relates an accurate assessment of the situation: the benefits of the kingdom are not constricted by external factors such as ethnicity, geography, and gender.[35] Further, the position of the narrative of the Syrophoenician woman between the two miraculous feedings (Mark 6:30–44; 8:1–10) turns her narrative into a type of interpretive lens through which the significance of the feeding narratives takes shape, showing that one of their imports is to reflect the lack of distinction between Jew and Gentile. The boundaries between the two groups have already been abolished in the course of Jesus's ministry.[36]

The divide between the twelve disciples and the Syrophoenician woman, however, does not revolve primarily around the distinction between their respective genders. As we have noted in previous chapters, Mark's portrait of discipleship involves more than a simple distinction between the genders of particular characters. The Syrophoenician woman becomes a narrative exemplar of discipleship neither because of nor in spite of her gender. Her discipleship is defined by her spoken embodiment of Jesus's λόγος. As with both Simon's mother-in-law (Mark 1:29–31) and the bleeding woman (Mark 5:25–34), the narrative of the Syrophoenician woman extends Mark's complex portrait of discipleship. Her individual narrative coheres with those earlier examples of narrative discipleship as part of the larger rhetorical device that Mark employs to create a spectrum of responses to Jesus. This Greek Syrophoenician woman joins Simon's mother-in-law and the bleeding woman as narrative illustrations of the reality and impact of Jesus's ministry.

The Syrophoenician woman's importance rests in her ability to speak the reality of the gospel. Her λόγος emphasizes that discipleship is defined in the first instance by an ability to stand in relationship with the two foci of Mark's narrative: Jesus and his gospel.[37] Theissen's influential socio-historical analysis is again helpful as he notes that the present narrative revolves

---

35. Collins, *Mark*, 365; Edwards, *Mark*, 217; Guelich, *Mark*, 389; Rhoads, "Jesus and the Syrophoenician Woman," 347.

36. Donahue and Harrington, *Gospel of Mark*, 238.

37. Malbon, "Fallible Followers," 46.

Spoken Discipleship (Mark 7)

around a potentially high-class Gentile woman prostrating herself before Jesus to obtain healing for another. The woman's posture of humility and concern for her daughter demonstrate that she understands the self-sacrifice required of Markan disciples (Mark 8:34–35). These characteristics are also illustrative of the inversion of status and holistic service that define Markan discipleship (Mark 9:35).[38] Although the position of the woman and her daughter as unclean Gentiles may initially suggest to Mark's audience that they are outsiders with respect to the kingdom, the outcome of their narrative creates a reversal of those expectations, reshaping the definition of discipleship from distinctions of ethnicity and gender to the parameters of the gospel itself. Jesus's λόγος is here embodied in the parable of the Syrophoenician woman whose narrative is a portrait of spoken discipleship.

CONCLUSION

The purpose of this chapter was to describe the way in which the narrative of the Syrophoenician woman (Mark 7:24–30) impacts Mark's wider portrayal of discipleship. I argued that the dramatic interaction between Jesus and the woman creates a portrait of *spoken discipleship*. The Syrophoenician woman's parable is a narrative speech-act that inhabits and explains the message of the gospel—Jesus's λόγος. Her parable is not simply a clever retort to Jesus's initial rejection; it is a description of the boundary-effacing nature of God's kingdom. The geographic setting of the narrative allows the Syrophoenician woman's experience to function as a living example of the reorientation inherent in the kingdom. As the divide between clean and unclean foods is set aside (Mark 7:1–23), so also is the divide between Jew and Gentile (Mark 7:24–30). The woman's parable embodies this inclusive kingdom reality. Although her introduction to the narrative positions her as an outsider to the kingdom, the narrative reversal inherent in her parable and the healing of her daughter invert our expectations about the identity of kingdom insiders. Mark's portrayal of the Syrophoenician woman establishes her as a kingdom participant and her unique exchange with Jesus provides a narrative example of spoken discipleship.

---

38. Cf. Betsworth, *Reign of God*, 142; Miller, *Women in Mark's Gospel*, 105.

5

Active Discipleship (Mark 12 and 14)

INTRODUCTION

GOD'S KINGDOM IS ROOTED in the narrative of Jesus. Mark's narrative Christology elucidates the way in which God works in and through Jesus to bring about the re-creation and restoration of the world. God's in-breaking kingdom is an active reality. Mark's narrative not only describes how Jesus embodies the kingdom in his own ministry but also demonstrates the way in which it creates a new reality that extends to humanity. In the context of Mark's Gospel we learn what it means to be a disciple of Jesus and his kingdom not through a structured set of logical propositions but through the narrative portrayal of Jesus and those who engage with him. There is a necessary connection in Mark's Gospel between Christology and discipleship. The way in which other participants in the narrative respond to and interact with Jesus creates the aretegenic framework of the Gospel. It is through these narrative portraits that Mark compels his audience toward virtue—toward embodied discipleship.

The narrative of Jesus is the paradigm within which Mark develops the pattern of narrative discipleship. This connection is no more transparent than in Jesus's declaration that discipleship requires a commitment to the reality of cross-bearing that defines his own ministry (Mark 8:34–38). Essential to Mark's wider portrait of discipleship are not only those characters who interact with and follow Jesus at distinct points of the narrative

Active Discipleship (Mark 12 and 14)

but also those who act in ways that reflect and embody Jesus's own sacrificial action. Those characters that reflect Jesus's sacrificial action within the Gospel serve as narrative examples for the audience of what it means to condition or shape one's life in terms of the kingdom that Jesus inaugurates and embodies. Mark's intentional description of the way in which these characters act provides the framework within which he can highlight key values of God's kingdom and essential characteristics of discipleship.

My intention in the present chapter is to describe how the portraits of two women—the poor widow (Mark 12:41–44) and the woman who anoints Jesus (Mark 14:3–9)—contribute to the definition of what it means to be a disciple by describing how their individual narratives reflect Mark's wider narrative of Jesus. We want to again answer the essential question that pervades this section of the book: how do these women function as narrative exemplars of Markan discipleship? The suggestion that I want to put forward is that these two narratives develop portraits of *active discipleship*. In particular, the way in which the actions of these two women embody larger dimensions of Mark's presentation of Jesus speaks to their importance in the wider narrative. To develop this thesis we will look first at the narrative of the poor widow (Mark 12:41–44) and then work through the narrative of the woman who anoints Jesus (Mark 14:3–9).

THE POOR WIDOW (MARK 12:41–44)

Within the structure of Mark's Gospel, Mark 11 constitutes an important transition. As the narrative shifts from Galilee to Jerusalem with Jesus's entry into the city (Mark 11:1–11), the cross becomes the primary focus of the story. The significant amount of hostility that Jesus encounters in Mark 11–12 becomes the primary catalyst for the final events of his life in Mark 14–15. The hostility that Jesus encounters in Mark 11–12 revolves primarily around the temple. From Jesus's initial entry into the temple courts (Mark 11:11) to his final exit (Mark 13:1) there is significant tension in the narrative. Jesus himself initiates the hostility that pervades the narrative with his dramatic demonstration in the temple courts (Mark 11:15–19).[1] The subsequent material in Mark 11:27–12:40 revolves around a series of disputes with various factions of the religious and political leadership in Jerusalem, as well as Jesus's own authoritative teaching against the temple and

---

1. On the function of the temple incident in Mark's Gospel, see Neville, *Vehement Jesus*, 119–29.

Part Two—Narratives *of* Discipleship

the religious leaders.[2] The initial portion of Jesus's eschatological speech in Mark 13 continues this persistent theme of hostility in its description of the temple's future destruction (Mark 13:1–2).[3] The extensive tension within Mark 11–13 emphasizes the distinct contrast that exists between the present kingdom and that which Jesus inaugurates in his incarnation, death, and resurrection. It is in the midst of this distinctly tense narrative that Jesus draws the attention of his disciples to a poor widow making a miniscule financial contribution to the temple treasury (Mark 12:41–44).

Narrative Disaster or Narrative Discipleship?

In the verses that immediately precede the short narrative of the poor widow Jesus urges the crowd to be aware of those scribes who live ostentatiously for their own gain (Mark 12:38–40). He notes that one of the ways these scribes support themselves is by devouring the houses of widows (Mark 12:40), a metaphorical way of describing the scribes' apparent coercion of the widows out of their resources for the scribes' own economic gain. The implied rebuke is that the frequent Old Testament prophetic admonitions against exploiting widows and orphans (e.g., Isa 1:17, 23; Jer 7:6; Ezek 22:7; Zech 7:10) have been ignored by certain segments of the religious leadership. Those with the ability to support these vulnerable individuals are intentionally trampling upon them. Within this context the question that emerges is what narrative function the story of the widow serves. Does Jesus draw attention to her as an example for the disciples to imitate or as a case study in the destructive practices of the scribes? Is her narrative one of praise or lament?

The large majority of Markan commentators understand Mark's portrayal of the widow as a positive example, with respect either to the nature and importance of financial giving or to Mark's wider portrait of discipleship.[4] In my estimation this latter suggestion offers the most constructive way forward in understanding the purpose of the widow's story. She is an important model in the narrative for understanding the shape of Markan

2. Cf. Marcus, *Mark*, 2:770.

3. On the function of Mark 13, see esp. Bolt, "Mark 13," 10–32; and Stein, *Jesus, the Temple, and the Coming of the Son of Man*.

4. See, e.g., Boring, *Mark*, 351–53; Collins, *Mark*, 586–90; Edwards, *Mark*, 379–82; France, *Gospel of Mark*, 492–93; Hooker, *Mark*, 296–97; Hurtado, *Mark*, 206–7; Marcus, *Mark*, 2:857–63; Moloney, *Gospel of Mark*, 245–48; Stein, *Mark*, 577–81.

Active Discipleship (Mark 12 and 14)

discipleship. Given the significant tension of the immediate context, however, not all interpreters understand the widow's narrative to be positive. In particular, Addison Wright's seminal article on the widow's narrative suggests that the immediate context, especially Mark 12:38–40 and 13:1–2, establishes her experience as an illustration of the corruption of the temple and the Jerusalem leadership.[5] In Wright's estimation, Jesus's hostile attitude toward the temple cult and his description of the temple's destruction in the surrounding verses do not allow for a positive reading of the widow's narrative. In Wright's words, the widow "had been taught and encouraged by religious leaders to donate as she does, and Jesus condemns the value system that motivates her action, and he condemns the people who conditioned her to do it."[6] Instead of being a narrative example of discipleship, her story is a dramatic narrative example of the disastrous way in which the scribes devour certain widows' resources.

To support his thesis Wright offers several arguments for the non-exemplary nature of Mark's portrayal of the widow. First, he argues against a perceived overemphasis in Markan scholarship on the financial aspect of the narrative, noting that "the story itself is not about the duty of almsgiving."[7] This is a constructive component of Wright's argument. The widow's narrative is not a paradigm for charitable contributions.[8] The contrast between her financial offering and the economic depravity of the scribes functions as the fulcrum upon which the narrative pivots, but the narrative itself functions more like an enacted parable.[9] The widow's financial contribution is representative of a wider thematic ideal. This is similar to our earlier discussion of Mark 1. Within that narrative Simon's mother-in-law (Mark 1:29–31) offered a particular type of service in response to Jesus's restorative action. The significance of her response, however, did not arise from the specific type of service she offered but from its confirmation of both her restored existence and her imitation of the ideal of service characteristic of Jesus's own ministry. Likewise, here in Mark 12 the narrative describes a specific form of giving, but the widow's contribution corresponds to a

---

5. Wright, "Widow's Mites," 256–65. See also Donahue and Harrington, *Gospel of Mark*, 365; Evans, *Mark 8:27–16:20*, 281–85; Sugirtharajah, "Widow's Mites," 42–43.

6. Wright, "Widow's Mites," 262.

7. Ibid., 259.

8. Cf. Gundry, *Mark*, 730.

9. For the argument that the narrative was originally a parable, see Dibelius, *From Tradition to Gospel*, 261; Marcus, *Mark*, 2:859; Nineham, *Mark*, 334–35.

Part Two—Narratives *of* Discipleship

wider ideal in the development of Mark's narrative. The impact of her story does not arise from the *financial* component of her contribution but rather from the *holistic* character of her action. The distinction that Jesus highlights for the disciples is not the reality of the widow's giving but its impact upon her livelihood.

That the central emphasis of the widow's narrative is not on the nature and importance of financial giving does not detract from her paradigmatic role in Mark's portrayal of the nature of discipleship. The widow is an example not with regard to fiscal responsibility or charitable contribution but with regard to her active sacrifice. Jesus's description of the woman's offering in Mark 12:44 as a contribution of "her whole life" (ὅλον τὸν βίον αὐτῆς) resonates with his description of his own ministry in Mark 10:45 as a giving up of "his life" (τὴν ψυχὴν αὐτοῦ). The vocabulary in each passage is distinct, but the thematic correlation is transparent.[10] Mark portrays the widow's action as a narrative example of the essential sacrificial nature of discipleship. Or, to use the intentional language of the present volume, Mark highlights the widow's action to create a portrait of narrative discipleship. Jesus's earlier description of the sacrificial nature of discipleship in Mark 8:35—"whoever loses their life (τὴν ψυχὴν αὐτοῦ) on account of me and the gospel will save it"—is here embodied in the woman's contribution. Within the development of Mark 11–15 the widow's action functions as a further movement toward the cross. She personifies the sacrificial ideal that Jesus describes in Mark 8 and embodies in Mark 14–15. Her action is a narrative portrayal of his future.

Second, Wright contends that the lack of originality in Jesus's statement is evidence for a non-exemplary interpretation of the widow's narrative. Given that there are other ancient examples that emphasize the value of offerings contributed by the poor (e.g., *Lev. Rab.* 3.5; *Midr. Psalms* 22.31; Xenophon, *Mem.* 1.3.3), Wright asserts that Jesus's "statement is simply one of those observations on life that needs to be said from time to time, and when it is said one would expect that virtually all would agree with it."[11] This seems to me to be a significant overstatement. Considering Wright's emphasis on the immediate context of the narrative, this argument overlooks the contrast between the scribes and the widow which constitutes the central emphasis of his article. Wright's assertion that the narrative

---

10. Interpreters of Mark's Gospel frequently note this thematic connection. For a constructive and representative example, see DiCicco, "What Can One Give," 441–49.

11. Wright, "Widow's Mites," 260.

Active Discipleship (Mark 12 and 14)

stresses lament is constructed precisely on the notion that the scribes do not recognize the value of the poor or that of their contribution. In that sense, Jesus's statement is contextually profound even if its sentiment is not historically unique.

Furthermore, the notion that the widow is an exemplar is profound given her explicit contrast with the extensive contributions of the wealthy. The verbal contrasts between Mark 12:41 and 12:42 create a deliberate antithesis between the many rich who offer large amounts (πολλοὶ πλούσιοι ἔβαλλον πολλά) and this single woman who offers only a miniscule contribution (μία χήρα πτωχὴ ἔβαλεν λεπτὰ δύο).[12] In spite of the limited financial value of her offering, the widow's contribution comprises the full extent of her monetary possessions. The remarkable reality that she contributes her entire livelihood is counter-intuitive. The audacity of her action is precisely the reason that Jesus commends it. Self-sacrifice to the point of death is the paradigm for both Markan Christology and Markan discipleship.

Third, both Wright and R. S. Sugirtharajah argue strongly against the exemplary function of the widow's narrative in light of the lack of an explicit reference by Jesus to this affect. According to Wright, "there is no invitation in the text to imitate the widow, no statement that Jesus looked on her and loved her, no command to go and do in like manner, no remark that she is not far from the kingdom. That her action is to be imitated may be implied, but it equally well may not be implied."[13] Likewise, Sugirtharajah argues "that there is no record of the widow ever becoming a follower of Jesus or joining one of the numerous bands of women's groups which fraternized with him, nor is there any specific request from Jesus to emulate her."[14] Both scholars are correct that there is no explicit call to imitate this poor widow. That same assertion, however, could be made of all of the female characters in Mark's Gospel. None of them are explicitly defined as disciples or objects of imitation. Even when aspects of the narratives of women are commended, such as the faith of the bleeding woman (Mark 5:34), there is no explicit declaration of the need for imitation. There are in fact no instances at the story level of Mark's Gospel in which someone who interacts with Jesus is explicitly positioned as a model for imitation. In contrast, Mark's portrayal of discipleship develops most clearly at the discourse level of the narrative. Mark's Gospel does not define discipleship

12. Marcus, *Mark*, 2:860.
13. Wright, "Widow's Mites," 259.
14. Sugirtharajah, "Widow's Mites," 42.

Part Two — Narratives *of* Discipleship

through explicit calls to imitate particular characters, but through an intentional connection of the portraits of those characters with specific aspects of Jesus's own life and ministry. Simply identifying the reality that Jesus does not explicitly call the disciples to imitate the widow does not negate the exemplary function of her narrative portrait that emerges in conjunction with the wider movement of Mark's Gospel.

More constructive is the analysis of Elizabeth Struthers Malbon, who highlights a number of narrative contexts with which the widow's story is connected as a means of demonstrating the exemplary nature of the widow in the wider movement of Mark's Gospel.[15] If we focus specifically on the immediate context of the narrative, then two important considerations arise. First, Mark's narration of Jesus's seated position (Mark 12:41), his calling of the disciples (Mark 12:42), and his use of the term "truly" (ἀμήν) to introduce his speech (Mark 12:43) suggest that the present narrative is to be understood as an example of Jesus's authoritative instruction.[16] In particular, Malbon directs attention to the three preceding instances in which Jesus calls his disciples in order to teach them—Mark 8:31–38; 9:35–37; 10:32–45.[17] These passages function as paradigmatic statements of Markan discipleship, with each establishing the interconnection between Jesus's experience and that of his disciples. The rhetorical significance of these earlier texts for the present narrative is that the woman's financial contribution represents a similar connection with Jesus. There is a narrative connection between her contribution of her whole life (ὅλον τὸν βίον αὐτῆς; Mark 12:44) and Jesus's contribution of his (τὴν ψυχὴν αὐτοῦ; Mark 10:45). Her action is an embodiment of the sacrificial nature of Jesus's ministry.

Second, Malbon also notes the important contrast between the widow and the scribes in the immediate context of Mark 12. The widow is not merely a victim of the scribes; she is their narrative foil. Her sacrificial contribution stands in direct contrast to the scribes' ostentatious behavior and economic depravity.[18] Mark's portrayal of the widow in this manner positions her not only as a positive example over against the scribes but also as one who corresponds with Jesus himself. Mark frequently places Jesus in direct contrast with the scribes (e.g., Mark 1:22; 2:6, 16; 3:22; 7:1–5; 11:18, 27–28; 12:35–40; 14:1), and they are one of the essential factions portrayed

15. Malbon, "Poor Widow," esp. 595–601.
16. Ibid., 600–601; cf. Donahue and Harrington, *Gospel of Mark*, 364.
17. Malbon, "Poor Widow," 600–601; cf. Collins, *Mark*, 589.
18. Malbon, "Poor Widow," 595.

Active Discipleship (Mark 12 and 14)

as responsible for orchestrating Jesus's arrest and execution (e.g., Mark 8:31; 10:33; 14:43, 53; 15:1, 31).[19] Wright is thus correct to note the overtly negative resonances of the widow's narrative, but as with Jesus, Mark portrays the widow's contribution as a paradoxical embodiment of the good news of God's in-breaking kingdom.[20] Her sacrifice of her whole life is a narrative demonstration of Jesus's own sacrificial act.

Our interpretation of Mark's portrayal of the widow can account for both the negative implications of the surrounding material and her position as an exemplar of discipleship. There is an emphasis in the immediate context on the disastrous tragedy inflicted on the widow by the scribes. Her poverty is an indictment of their lack of care for the vulnerable. But the widow's poverty and audacious financial contribution are not an indictment of her. In spite of her position, she gives her life. Consequently, the widow's action does not serve merely as an example of Jesus's negative view of the temple and of the religious leaders, but also as a paradigm for a specific dimension of Mark's portrait of discipleship—sacrificial action. With regard to the progression of the narrative, the fact that Jesus does not explicitly describe the widow with the term "disciple" does not detract from her importance.[21] In contrast, the essential reality is that Mark narrates her story as a portrait of the type of holistic sacrificial action required of those who desire to follow the crucified Christ. The widow's discipleship is not explicit but *narratival*. Its importance is rooted in the aretegenic function of the Gospel.

Holistic Action

We have already seen that there is a strong thematic connection between the woman's sacrificial contribution (Mark 12:44) and Jesus's description of his own ministry (Mark 10:45). One further consideration may be put forward as a way to establish the exemplary function of the widow's narrative in Mark's Gospel, namely the holistic nature of her action. That Mark informs the audience that the woman still possessed two coins (Mark 12:42) may suggest that she contributed more than she needed to.[22] Indeed, there seems to be a clear contextual emphasis in Mark 12:44 on the fact

19. Ibid., 595–96.
20. Cf. France, *Gospel of Mark*, 489–50.
21. Cf. Boring, *Mark*, 352.
22. Cf. Hooker, *Mark*, 296.

Part Two—Narratives *of* Discipleship

that the widow contributes her *whole* livelihood (ὅλον τὸν βίον αὐτῆς). She did not simply give a portion of her remaining financial resources, but contributed everything she had (πάντα ὅσα εἶχεν ἔβαλεν). Jesus's description of the widow's offering in this way harks back to his interaction with the rich man (Mark 10:17–31).[23] In response to the rich man's inquiry about how he might inherit eternal life and his affirmation of his faithfulness to the commandments, Jesus exhorts him to divest himself of all of his resources—to sell everything he had (ὅσα ἔχεις πώλησον; Mark 10:21). The man responds by departing solemnly, unable to come to terms with the extensive commitment required in following Jesus. In distinct contrast, the poor widow offers the entirety of her resources in spite of her extensive poverty. Her contribution is judged not by its monetary value but by its holistic character. Her narrative constitutes a paradigm of the holistic commitment required by the revaluation of reality brought about in Jesus's inauguration of a new kingdom.[24]

Mark's emphasis on the *holistic* nature of the widow's action also reverberates in the more immediate chamber of Mark 12. In stark contrast to those scribes who devour widows' houses, Mark earlier narrates the story of an individual scribe who approaches Jesus to inquire about the identification of the greatest commandment (Mark 12:28–34). Jesus's response to this scribe's inquiry exhibits a specific focus on the holistic nature of discipleship reflected in the widow's contribution. He exhorts the scribe concerning the need to "love the Lord your God with your whole heart (ὅλης τῆς καρδίας) and with your whole soul (ὅλης τῆς ψυχῆς) and with your whole mind (ὅλης τῆς διανοίας) and with your whole strength (ὅλης τῆς ἰσχύος)" (Mark 12:30). The scribe then echoes the holistic emphasis of Jesus's answer, affirming the need "to love [God] with one's whole heart (ὅλης τῆς καρδίας) and whole understanding (ὅλης τῆς συνέσεως) and whole strength (ὅλης τῆς ἰσχύος)" (Mark 12:33).[25] This particular scribe's understanding of the holistic nature of Jesus's message sets him apart from the negative resonances of the surrounding context. His interaction with Jesus does not result in conflict, but with Jesus's declaration that his perception of reality reflects an accurate description of the nature of God's kingdom

---

23. Cf. Beavis, "Women as Models of Faith," 6; Marcus, *Mark*, 2:862; Miller, *Women in Mark's Gospel*, 117–19; Moloney, *Gospel of Mark*, 247–48; Stein, *Mark*, 578; Williams, *Other Followers*, 178.

24. So too France, *Gospel of Mark*, 489–90.

25. See esp. Williams, *Other Followers*, 176–77.

Active Discipleship (Mark 12 and 14)

(Mark 12:34). In the midst of the hostility and tension of Mark 11–13, these two individuals function as paradoxical exemplars of the holistic commitment required by Mark's portrait of discipleship—the scribe through his unexpected affirmation of Jesus's teaching and the poor widow through her financial sacrifice.[26]

The paradoxical extravagance of the widow's holistic contribution points to a further connection between her narrative and the wider movement of Mark's Gospel. The widow's narrative likely represents an expression of the Markan ideal that "many who are first will be last, and the last first" (Mark 10:31).[27] The stark contrast between the woman's action and that of the surrounding wealthy patrons demonstrates this important note of reversal in Mark's narrative. The kingdom embodied in Jesus's ministry abandons the perspective of importance inherent in the world and explicit in the ostentatious behavior of the scribes in the immediate context.[28] The significance of the widow's contribution does not stem from its economic value but from its orientation toward the ideals of Jesus's new kingdom. In the words of Susan Miller, "the willingness to give everything cuts across the values of the world, which are concerned with status and power. The world is concerned with survival, whereas the gospel is concerned with the paradox that saving life involves giving life away (8.34–38)."[29] The widow's action functions as a parabolic expression of the holistic and sacrificial nature of Christian discipleship. Within the context of Mark 12:41–44 the widow's offering is extravagant because it represents her entire economic livelihood. Within the context of Mark's narrative her offering is extravagant because it represents the holistic commitment of Jesus's own sacrifice. It embodies Jesus's past teaching and points toward the cross.[30] Her narrative action is a paradigm for discipleship in light of its cohesion with the holistic and sacrificial reality of Jesus's narrative.

THE WOMAN WHO ANOINTS JESUS (MARK 14:3-9)

Jesus's departure from the temple after the narrative of the poor widow (Mark 12:41–44) is followed by his longest speech in the Gospel. The

26. Cf. Williams, *Other Followers*, 178.
27. Cf. France, *Gospel of Mark*, 493; Malbon, "Poor Widow," 600.
28. Cf. France, *Gospel of Mark*, 490.
29. Miller, *Women in Mark's Gospel*, 118.
30. DiCicco, "What Can One Give," 442.

Part Two—Narratives *of* Discipleship

eschatological speech of Mark 13 portrays the imminent tension that the disciples will face in light of the shape and reality of Jesus's ministry. The hostility which Jesus encounters in Jerusalem in Mark 11–12 and the stark reality of the cross manifest in Mark 14–15 here become the paradigm for Jesus's followers. His sacrifice will be embodied in that of the community. Given the close proximity of her story, the poor widow functions as a narrative precursor for this paradigm.[31] She models the way in which disciples will be called to divest themselves of their lives. When the focus of the Gospel returns to Jesus's passion in Mark 14 the portrait of another woman emerges in the narrative. While Jesus reclines for a meal in the home of Simon the leper in Bethany an anonymous woman enters the room and proceeds to pour out an extravagantly priced perfume on his head (Mark 14:3). Her action functions in the wider narrative as an *inclusio* or bookend with the narrative of the poor widow, bracketing off Jesus's extensive speech in Mark 13.[32] Out of their diverse situations—the widow from her poverty and this anonymous woman from her wealth—they embody a narrative connection with Jesus's cross.[33]

Foolish Waste or Faithful Discipleship?

In the immediate context of Mark 14 the woman's extravagant action is vehemently contested by some of the others present at the meal. Both the woman and her objectors remain anonymous in Mark's narrative, but the dividing line between them is transparent. The voiced opposition revolves primarily around the woman's apparent waste of a valuable resource. Mark's extensive description of the perfume in his introduction of the woman highlights its significant value (Mark 14:3). He describes it as being comprised of nard, an expensive substance derived from a plant in India and imported into the region.[34] Those opposed to the woman's action suggest that the perfume could have been sold for over three hundred denarii (Mark 14:5). Given the note in Matt 20:2 that a denarius represented the typical daily wage for an agricultural worker in the first century CE, the

---

31. Malbon, "Minor Characters," 78.

32. Beavis, *Mark*, 209; Hooker, *Mark*, 327; Malbon, "Fallible Followers," 39; Moloney, *Gospel of Mark*, 281; Stein, *Mark*, 638; Williams, *Other Followers*, 50–51.

33. The following material resonates strongly with and builds upon the insightful essay by Barton, "Mark as Narrative," 230–34.

34. See, e.g., Stein, *Mark*, 633.

Active Discipleship (Mark 12 and 14)

contents of the woman's jar appear to have been worth the equivalent of approximately a year's wages. Her unexpected—and perhaps uninvited—act of extravagance functions as a dramatic incursion into Mark's narrative.

As Eugene Boring notes, it is essential for our understanding of both the vehemence of the objection and the decisive nature of Jesus's counter-response that we grasp the radical nature of the woman's action.[35] She does not merely anoint Jesus's head in a manner that might be recognized as a normal act of hospitality in the ancient world; rather, she shatters (συντρίψασα) her alabaster jar and pours out (κατέχεεν) the entirety of its contents (Mark 14:3).[36] Although it is sometimes suggested that breaking the alabaster jar would have been the only means for the woman to procure the perfume, there appears to be neither archaeological nor literary evidence to support this notion. In contrast, these small jars of perfume were often sealed with a piece of cloth, parchment, or papyrus. This method of sealing would enable the perfume to be used slowly and in moderation.[37] The woman's action stands in stark contrast to this standard practice. She acts not with cautious reservation but with comprehensive finality.

The extreme nature of the woman's action explains the decisive response it receives from both the anonymous objectors and Jesus. The opposition to the woman's action does not develop calmly. Mark's claim that the woman's opponents were "indignant amongst themselves" (Mark 14:4) is not suggestive of merely a private grievance. Parallel uses of the phrase "amongst themselves" (πρὸς ἑαυτούς) in other sections of the Gospel suggest a more deliberate and vocal outrage (cf. Mark 1:27; 10:26; 11:31; 12:7; 16:3). The heightened emotion of the scene persists in the subsequent note that her opponents openly rebuked her (Mark 14:5).[38] Their vocal opposition to her perceived misuse of a valuable resource is portrayed in clear contrast to her own narrative silence. Despite the extremely vocal vehemence that marks their objection, the narrative does not betray any notion that the opposition is disingenuous. Their stated concern for the poor coheres well with Jesus's prior exhortation to the rich man to sell his property and give the proceeds to the poor (Mark 10:21), as well as with the note that the present scene occurs in chronological proximity to the Festival of Passover (Mark 14:1), in which giving to the poor was a traditional emphasis. These

---

35. Boring, *Mark*, 382.
36. On the historical nature of the woman's action, see Collins, *Mark*, 641–42.
37. See esp. Marcus, *Mark*, 2:934; cf. France, *Gospel of Mark*, 552.
38. France, *Gospel of Mark*, 553; cf. Bayer, *Markus*, 492.

Part Two — Narratives *of* Discipleship

contextual associations may suggest that the opposition to the woman's action is in fact valid.[39]

Despite the positive motivation behind the opposition to the woman's action, Jesus rejects its potential validity immediately. In response to their verbal abuse, Jesus speaks decisively in the woman's favor (Mark 14:6), commanding that she be left alone and questioning the negative treatment directed at her. He describes the action not as the waste of a valuable resource but as a "good work" (καλὸν ἔργον). Furthermore, Jesus shifts the opponents' concern about the poor toward a question of temporality: "You will have the poor with you always and whenever you want you are able to do good for them, but you will not always have me" (Mark 14:7). Jesus's assertion does not reflect a lack of ethical concern for the poor. The resonances between his statement and Deut 15:11—"There will always be poor people in the land"—suggest rather that he understands responsibility for the poor to be a permanent obligation.[40] Jesus portrays the woman's action not as something in contrast to engaging with the social reality of poverty but rather as an appropriate act of devotion given the limited time frame of his own presence. A similar sentiment develops in Mark 2:18–22, in which Jesus interprets his disciples' lack of fasting in connection with the unique reality of his own presence. Jesus's focus is christological. He regards the woman's action as a beautiful representation of the necessity for complete devotion to himself.[41]

The comprehensive finality of the woman's action pushes Jesus's commendation of it further in Mark 14:8. He interprets the extensive nature of her action neither as a delayed measure of hospitality nor as a simple act of devotion. Rather, Jesus asserts that her action is part of the preparation for his burial. That is, he interprets it as an action that recognizes the imminent reality of his death. It is important to note with Morna Hooker that it was common practice in the ancient world for jars used to anoint the dead "to be broken and left in the tomb."[42] The finality of the woman's action may point to her own understanding of the reality and necessity of the subsequent events portrayed in the narrative. Indeed, as Francis Moloney argues,

---

39. Cf. Collins, *Mark*, 642.
40. Marcus, *Mark*, 2:941; Stein, *Mark*, 634.
41. Hurtado, *Mark*, 230.
42. Hooker, *Mark*, 329; cf. Nineham, *Mark*, 374.

Active Discipleship (Mark 12 and 14)

the woman "is the only one at the gathering who has correctly read the events surrounding Jesus's presence in the vicinity of Jerusalem."[43]

Within the development of Mark's Gospel, however, the contextual emphasis lies on Jesus's interpretation of the woman's action. Her action is essential in light of its direct connection with the climatic events of the narrative—Jesus's death, burial, and resurrection. This connection is born out in the thematic similarity that exists between the present narrative and that of the poor widow. In the same way that Jesus describes the financial contribution of the poor widow as a donation of everything she had (πάντα ὅσα εἶχεν; Mark 12:44), he asserts that the anonymous woman's action constitutes a holistic contribution—"What she had, she did" (ὃ ἔσχεν ἐποίησεν; Mark 14:8).[44] The somewhat unusual phrasing in Mark 14:8 creates a link between the two narratives. Each woman offers a holistic contribution which Jesus then interprets in connection with his death. The poor widow's offering embodies the self-sacrifice inherent in the cross and the woman's anointing confirms its forthcoming reality.

The narrative emphasis on Jesus's death is highlighted further by Mark's placement of the story in the present context. The woman's narrative functions not only as the second half of an *inclusio* with Mark 12:38–44, it functions as another example of a Markan intercalation—a "literary sandwich" in which one story is inserted into another to create a mutually interpretive framework.[45] The woman's act of devotion is inserted into a narrative about the plot to arrest and kill Jesus. The preceding material narrates the way in which the chief priests and the scribes are scheming against Jesus (Mark 14:1–2), while the immediately subsequent material provides the needed means for their plan with the narration of Judas's betrayal (Mark 14:10–11). The contrasts between the narratives are extensive and well documented.[46] Instead of preparing for the Passover, some of the leaders in Jerusalem are seeking a way to destroy Jesus. In contrast, outside

---

43. Moloney, *Gospel of Mark*, 281; cf. Senior, *Passion of Jesus*, 44–48.

44. See also Donahue and Harrington, *Gospel of Mark*, 388; Edwards, *Mark*, 415; Hooker, *Mark*, 330; Marcus, *Mark*, 2:936, 941; Miller, *Women in Mark's Gospel*, 117; Strauss, *Mark*, 608–9.

45. See Shepherd, "Markan Intercalation," 522–40.

46. See, e.g., Barton, "Mark as Narrative," 231; Bayer, *Markus*, 491–94; Black, *Mark*, 283–84; Broadhead, *Prophet, Son, Messiah*, 29–50; Donahue and Harrington, *Gospel of Mark*, 390; Edwards, *Mark*, 411; Grassi, "Secret Heroine," 11–13; Hurtado, *Mark*, 229; Kelhoffer, "A Tale of Two Markan Characterizations," 87–89; Malbon, "Fallible Followers," 39–40; Stein, *Mark*, 637–38; Williams, *Other Followers*, 181.

Part Two—Narratives *of* Discipleship

of Jerusalem in Bethany, an anonymous woman destroys an expensive alabaster jar in devotion to him. Likewise, while an unnamed woman enters unexpectedly into the house to sacrifice an extraordinarily expensive jar of perfume, one of Jesus's closest followers leaves the house to sacrifice Jesus for money. Mark intertwines these scenes with an intentional focus on the passion narrative that will emerge in the subsequent scenes of the Gospel.

The specific contrast with Judas highlights that the woman's extraordinary action is not merely a narrative precursor to Jesus's death. It also functions as a narrative portrait of discipleship. Stephen Barton has stated the point in the strongest terms by arguing that Mark casts "the anonymous woman as a Christ-figure. Her extravagant love expressed in an act of self-giving which provokes conflict, is an anticipation in the narrative of what will happen to Jesus himself."[47] To state it another way, the woman's action provides a narrative outline for Jesus's ministry and, consequently, discipleship. Mark's presentation of discipleship is rooted in the unexpected necessity of cruciform self-sacrifice (Mark 8:34). The contrast between the woman's action and Judas's betrayal speaks to the radical inversion of priorities embodied in the cruciform nature of discipleship. The woman's importance is tied not to her identity but to the correlation of her action with Jesus. Although Judas maintains a higher narrative status as one of Jesus's closest followers, his actions fail to model the self-sacrifice inherent in Jesus's ministry.[48] Like the anonymous women who have preceded her in the Gospel, Mark inserts the narrative of this particular woman to highlight a key christological element of discipleship.

Given the strong contrast between the woman's action and that of one of Jesus's closest followers, it also becomes clear that Mark frames the entire passion narrative with portraits of faithful women who function as narrative foils for those portrayed as Jesus's primary disciples (Mark 14:3–9; 15:40–41, 47; 16:1–8). While Judas betrays Jesus (Mark 14:10–11, 43–45) and the rest of the disciples abandon him (Mark 14:50–52, 66–72), these women anchor the narrative. The women in Mark 15–16 are the only people in the narrative who witness the climatic events of the Gospel, and it is this woman in Mark 14 who pushes the narrative forward by preparing Jesus for the cross. In light of the apparently negative ending of the Gospel in Mark 16:8 it will be necessary to explain Mark's portrayal of the women in Mark

---

47. Barton, "Mark as Narrative," 232; cf. Miller, *Women in Mark's Gospel*, 138; Vanhoozer, *Faith Speaking Understanding*, 44.

48. Barton, "Mark as Narrative," 233.

Active Discipleship (Mark 12 and 14)

15–16 in more detail in the next chapter, but at this stage we can see that the two references to Jesus's anointing in Mark 14:3 and 16:1 constitute another narrative *inclusio*, bracketing off the primary scenes of Jesus's passion.[49] Mark's intentional positioning of the woman's story at this key point in the narrative emphasizes the positive nature of her portrayal. She embodies the active discipleship portrayed in the narrative of the poor widow in Mark 12 and foreshadows the cruciform discipleship that will be portrayed in the narrative of the named women in Mark 15–16.

Remembered Action

The dramatic action of the woman in Mark 14:3—which John Calvin refers to as "an extraordinary performance"[50]—develops in close connection with a number of elements in the wider narrative of Mark's Gospel. Her story is a narrative example of discipleship and a key lens through which Mark's passion narrative develops. We have seen that her story forms the second half of an *inclusio* around the eschatological speech in Mark 13 with the narrative of the poor widow (Mark 12:41–44). We noted that her narrative is the central portion of a dramatic intercalation—a narrative sandwich—contrasting her action with that of the chief priests, scribes, and Judas. And, we have argued that her narrative serves as the first half of an *inclusio* around the crucial events of the passion narrative in Mark 14–15 with the portrayal of the women in Mark 15–16. Within the structure of Mark's Gospel, his presentation of this anonymous woman's dramatic action plays a significant role in binding elements of the narrative together.[51] It is crucial to note, however, that the importance of this woman's action is not limited by the boundaries of Mark's Gospel. The portrait of her discipleship becomes intricately connected with the wider narrative of Christianity with Jesus's astounding assertion in Mark 14:9: "Truly I say to you, wherever the gospel is proclaimed in the whole world, what she has done will also be told in memory of her."

In the introduction to perhaps the most important work on feminist readings of Scripture, Elisabeth Schüssler Fiorenza argues that Christian tradition has, in contrast to Jesus's assertion, forgotten this anonymous

---

49. Sabin, *Reopening the Word*, 196; cf. Bauckham, *Gospel Women*, 293; Williams, *Other Followers*, 51.

50. Calvin, *Harmony of the Evangelists*, 3:188.

51. Cf. Malbon, "Minor Characters," 76–77.

Part Two—Narratives *of* Discipleship

woman. She notes that, "the name of the betrayer is remembered, but the name of the faithful disciple is forgotten because she was a woman."[52] Although much of Schüssler Fiorenza's subsequent material is thoroughly insightful, this introductory analysis is, in my estimation, a *non sequitur*. Even if later Christian tradition has been negligent in its emphasis of this woman's story, her anonymity in the present context is neither a sign of Markan neglect nor of gender bias. Her anonymity positions her alongside the anonymous women portrayed earlier in Mark's narrative—Simon's mother-in-law, the bleeding woman, the Syrophoenician woman, and the poor widow—whose portraits all embody essential characteristics of Markan discipleship. Consequently, the analysis of Miller is more constructive: "The lack of information about the woman . . . enables her to be portrayed as a representative of humanity and as a role model within the community."[53] In contrast to the notion that her anonymity is an ironic discounting of her importance because of her gender, it serves as one of the narrative catalysts for her remembered position in the wider proclamation of the gospel. Her anonymity heightens the contrast between her story and that of Judas, allowing it to serve as a narrative example of the unexpected reversal that characterizes Mark's presentation of God's in-breaking kingdom.

The potential misunderstanding that the woman's anonymity is a by-product of her gender also detracts from its narrative function in the present context. Jesus's declaration at the conclusion of Mark 14:9 is that the woman's *action*—not her *identity*—is the aspect of her story which will be remembered in the proclamation of the gospel.[54] Her anonymity allows for her action to be the central component of the narrative. Jesus's emphasis on the woman's action draws attention back to his interpretation of its purpose. Her extravagant action embodies the holistic commitment required of faithful discipleship and looks forward to the reality of the cross in its preparation of Jesus for his burial (Mark 14:8). Her action functions as a narrative portrait of the cruciform reality of Mark's Gospel.[55] It is because of this thematic connection with Mark's wider emphasis on the cross that

---

52. Schüssler Fiorenza, *In Memory of Her*, xiii; cf. Donahue and Harrington, *Gospel of Mark*, 391; Getty-Sullivan, *Women in the New Testament*, 217.

53. Miller, *Women in Mark's Gospel*, 139.

54. Cf. Barton, "Mark as Narrative," 233; Miller, *Women in Mark's Gospel*, 139; Moloney, *Gospel of Mark*, 282; Stein, *Mark*, 635–36.

55. Cf. Evans, *Mark*, 362; Hooker, *Mark*, 327–28.

Active Discipleship (Mark 12 and 14)

the woman's action becomes a persistent memorial for her (εἰς μνημόσυνον αὐτῆς) in the ongoing proclamation of the gospel.

Joel Marcus draws insightful connections between Mark's specific terminology of memory in the present context and the language of several funerary inscriptions and gravestones from the ancient world.[56] His theological assessment of the connection is worth quoting at length:

> This formula fits into the general context, in which Jesus has been talking about his own death and burial; in an unexpected twist, however, he now speaks of a memorial not for himself but for the woman who has just anointed him. This twist points to the surprising reversal implicit in the conclusion of the subsection: the burial of Jesus will not be an end but a beginning. He will not require a memorial, because he will not remain dead, and the power that his resurrection will unleash in the cosmos will transform the deeds of those who serve him into episodes in the worldwide triumph of the good news.[57]

The thrust of Marcus's argument is that the emphasis on death that pervades this section of Mark's Gospel, both in the surrounding narrative about the plot against Jesus and in Jesus's interpretation of the woman's extravagant action, remains central in Jesus's final assertion in Mark 14:9. The remarkable component of the narrative, however, is that the woman's act of death becomes intimately related with the proclamation of the gospel—an act of resurrection. Her action is not only a narrative precursor to Jesus's death but also an example of remembered participation in the message and reality of the resurrection.

That the woman's action is positioned in the narrative as if it were her own funerary inscription (εἰς μνημόσυνον αὐτῆς) represents a crucial reminder of the close connection that exists between Markan Christology and Markan discipleship. Mark's persistent narrative movement toward the cross and his extensive focus on the reality of the passion point to the notion that Jesus's identity can only be known in the cross.[58] Neither the narrative of the resurrection nor that of the gospel leaves the deadly nature of the cross behind. Jesus's crucified existence is an essential part of the narrative. It is the *crucified one* (τὸν ἐσταυρωμένον) who will meet both the women and the departed disciples in Galilee (Mark 16:6–7). That the cross

---

56. Marcus, *Mark*, 2:937.
57. Ibid., 2:942; cf. Broadhead, *Prophet, Son, Messiah*, 34.
58. See esp. Hurtado, "Following Jesus," 25–27.

remains a perpetual aspect of Jesus's identity gives further weight to his own declaration about the reality of discipleship. Taking up one's cross and being defined by the cruciform identity of Jesus's ministry (Mark 8:34) is not merely an aspect of discipleship in the interim between Jesus's resurrection and return. The life of discipleship is both cruciform and resurrected. It embodies both Jesus's resurrected life and his sacrificial death. This is, in my mind, the essential reason that Mark narrates Jesus's commendation of the woman's action. The active discipleship she demonstrates in her sacrificial extravagance focuses the narrative on the forthcoming reality of Jesus's death. And its specific correlation with Jesus's death allows it to be transformed into a perpetual memorial to the reversal brought about in Jesus's resurrection. Resurrected life arises from sacrificial death, and active discipleship is characterized by an embodiment of both realities.

CONCLUSION

The purpose of this chapter was to describe the way in which the narratives of the poor widow (Mark 12:41–44) and the woman who anoints Jesus (Mark 14:3–9) contribute to Mark's wider portrayal of discipleship. I argued that Mark's intentional narration of these two distinct women creates a portrait of *active discipleship*. Mark highlights the way in which each woman's unique action embodies the sacrificial reversal inherent in God's new kingdom. Each woman offers a narrative portrait of the kingdom reality of Mark's Gospel—the poor widow through her holistic contribution and the anonymous woman through her remembered extravagance. Their actions are not merely narrated examples of their own faithfulness but rather narrative examples of the connection between Markan Christology and Markan discipleship. The narratives do not point to the necessity of embodying the specific actions of each woman—financial contribution and extravagant anointing. Indeed, the subsequent destruction of the temple and Jesus's resurrection mean that both actions are now non-repeatable events. In contrast, the emphasis of each narrative is on the way in which each woman actively participates in the paradigm of discipleship created by Mark's portrait of Jesus. These women provide narrative portraits of active discipleship in their reflection of Jesus.

6

Cruciform Discipleship (Mark 15–16)

INTRODUCTION

GOD'S KINGDOM IS DEFINED by the reality of Jesus's death and resurrection. Mark constructs his Gospel with a specific narrative focus on these twin realities. Interpreters often point to Martin Kähler's famous assertion that the Gospels are "passion narratives with extended introductions."[1] Although Kähler's words are an overstated caricature of the contents of the Gospels, they rightly emphasize the centrality of Jesus's death and resurrection in Mark's narrative. Mark's dramatic presentation of these climatic events highlights his understanding of Jesus as the Son of God—the one in whom and through whom God's kingdom is established.

As with the rest of the Gospel, the nature of Markan discipleship is thoroughly rooted in the narrative of Jesus's death and resurrection. Mark's narration of these dramatic events serves not merely as a historical account of Jesus of Nazareth but also as an aretegenic instrument to shape the response of his audience. The cross is not only the primary outline for Jesus's identity but also for that of his followers. The paradoxical inversion of power and authority that characterizes God's in-breaking kingdom is not diminished by the reality of the resurrection. In contrast, Jesus's resurrection confirms that the cross defines God's kingdom and those who desire to participate in it. The climactic events of Mark's Gospel compel the audience

1. Kähler, *So-Called Historical Jesus*, 80n11.

Part Two—Narratives *of* Discipleship

to respond—to become disciples who embody the narrative of the crucified one (Mark 16:6).

My intention in the present chapter is to show how the portrait of the three named women in Mark 15–16—Mary Magdalene, Mary, the mother of James the younger and Joses, and Salome—contributes to the intentional connection that Mark creates between Jesus's cross and discipleship.[2] My suggestion is that these women serve as narrative representatives of *cruciform discipleship*. The first step in developing this thesis involves a reexamination of the enigmatic conclusion of Mark's Gospel.[3] Most important is a reevaluation of Mark 16:8, which seemingly describes the women as fleeing from the tomb in fearful and disobedient silence and failing to report the message of restoration offered in light of Jesus's resurrection. In contrast to the frequent negative assessment of their portrait, I offer a positive assessment of the women as narrative witnesses of the climactic events of the Gospel.[4] The second step is to describe how Mark's portrayal of the women as faithful witnesses coordinates with his wider emphasis on the centrality of the cross.

THE NAMED WOMEN (MARK 15-16)

The majority of the women who populate Mark's narrative are anonymous. Prior to Mark 15 the only named women in the Gospel are Mary (Mark 6:3) and Herodias (Mark 6:14–29). The contrast between Mark's isolated references to named women and his general practice of leaving women unnamed makes the introduction of three named women in the final scenes of the Gospel unique. Both the late introduction of these named women into the narrated events of the story and the explicit repetition of their identification three times (Mark 15:40–41, 47; 16:1) emphasizes their distinct

---

2. Although the specific identities of the women are not unimportant, I am concerned primarily with the literary function of the women as a group. For a concise introduction to the historical identity of the women, see Collins, *Mark*, 774–75.

3. For a survey of the way in which scholars have understood the ending of Mark's Gospel, see Driggers, *Following God through Mark*, 86–96; and Williams, "Literary Approaches," 21–35. I assume that Mark 16:8 represents the intentional ending of the Gospel. For a survey of the text-critical issues, see Metzger, *Textual Commentary*, 102–6; and Stein, "The Ending of Mark," 79–98. For a substantive argument in support of Mark 16:9–20 as the original ending, see Lunn, *The Original Ending of Mark*.

4. The positive assessment of the women developed here is dependent in large part on the constructive proposal advanced in Hurtado, "Women, the Tomb," 427–50.

position in the Gospel.[5] Given the intentional way that Mark crafts his narrative—in terms of both story and discourse—the portrait he develops of these women is unlikely to be haphazard. While the twelve disciples have abandoned Jesus in dramatic fashion (Mark 14:50-52; 66-72), these women enter the narrative to witness its climactic events—Jesus's death, burial, and resurrection.

Perhaps more striking with respect to the progression of the narrative is that Mark introduces these three named women alongside a larger group of anonymous women (Mark 15:40-41). Despite their absence from the narrated events of the Gospel up to this point, Mark asserts that this wider group of women had followed and served Jesus since he was in Galilee.[6] The explicit connection of the three named women with this larger group positions them as its narrative representatives. Their actions reflect the characterization of the whole group. Mark's intentionally belated introduction of these women into the narrated events of the Gospel draws together the analogous portraits of anonymous women spread throughout the narrative. With respect to the story of Mark's Gospel, these women are named representatives of the wider anonymous group of women introduced in the immediate context of Mark 15-16. With respect to the discourse of Mark's Gospel, these women are narrative representatives of a unique character group that stretches from Mark 1 to 16. In conjunction with the climactic narrative events of the Gospel—Jesus's embodiment of God's kingdom in his death and resurrection—Mark completes the trajectory of discipleship embodied in the narrative portraits of the women.

The Narrative Trajectory of the Named Women

Interpreters of Mark's Gospel often connect the narrative portrait of the named women in Mark 15-16 with the negative trajectory of Mark's characterization of the twelve disciples. Parallels between the two groups are identified both in Mark's characterization of each group—such as a perceived narrative arc from faithfulness to failure—and in specific linguistic connections that exist between the story of these women and the disciples.[7] The portraits of the two groups, however, are not uniform. There is

---

5. Cf. ibid., 429. On the historical significance of Mark's naming the women in the present context, see ibid., 429-31.

6. Cf. Malbon, "Minor Characters," 60-61.

7. See, e.g., Kelhoffer, "A Tale of Two Markan Characterizations," 85-98; Malbon,

Part Two—Narratives of Discipleship

both a rhetorical connection between the disciples and the named women, and a rhetorical contrast between them.

For example, there is a clear connection between Mark's initial description of the women as watching Jesus's crucifixion "from a distance" (ἀπὸ μακρόθεν; Mark 15:40) and his use of the same phrase to describe Peter's position at Jesus's trial (Mark 14:54).[8] To claim, however, that Mark's description of the women's geographic distance from the cross parallels the negative connotations implied in Peter's portrait does not account for the narrative movement of each scene.[9] The negative assessment of Peter's position becomes clear only in connection with the wider context concerning his three-fold denial (Mark 14:66–72) and his subsequent physical absence from the narrative. Peter begins the scene by following Jesus "from a distance" and then eventually moves *farther* away from him. In contrast, Mark portrays the women at the crucifixion observing events from a similar distance but then develops their *continued* presence in the narrative.[10] The women follow Jesus's body to its burial site (Mark 15:47) and then return on the first day of the week in an apparent demonstration of their continued devotion (Mark 16:1). The linguistic connection between the

---

"Fallible Followers," 29–48; Moloney, *Gospel of Mark*, 349; Tolbert, *Sowing the Gospel*, 288–99.

8. E.g., Malbon, "Fallible Followers," 43; Moloney, *Gospel of Mark*, 332, 348; Williams, *Other Followers*, 188.

9. See Miller, *Women in Mark's Gospel*, 168. Miller highlights both the positive behavior of the women and the negative dimensions of the phrase. Yet, if Mark's use of the phrase is seen as an intended contrast with the narrative of Peter, then the ambiguity is avoided.

10. This contrast also qualifies Mark's potential allusion to Psalm 37 LXX in his use of the phrase "from a distance" (ἀπὸ μακρόθεν). If Mark intends to establish a connection between Jesus's passion narrative and the plight of the righteous sufferer in the psalm, whose closest companions abandon him (καὶ οἱ ἔγγιστά μου ἀπὸ μακρόθεν ἔστησαν; Ps 37:12 LXX), then the apparent force of the linguistic connection again develops a contrast between those in the psalm who stand idly by (like Peter in Mark 14:54) and the women in Mark who maintain an active presence in the narrative (see Miller, *Women in Mark's Gospel*, 160–61). The women's continued presence in the narrative also supports France's view that the phrase "from a distance" distinguishes the women *positively* from the mockers and soldiers who are in the immediate presence of Jesus's cross (*Gospel of Mark*, 663n79). Bauckham also suggests that their distance may stem from the possibility that the Roman soldiers would have prohibited them from approaching the cross more closely (*Gospel Women*, 293n94). Schüssler Fiorenza argues that their distance from the cross suggests the reality of their association with Jesus and the potential political danger of being associated with him (*In Memory of Her*, 320; cf. Miller, "Women Characters," 188–89).

Cruciform Discipleship (Mark 15-16)

two passages is indeed important, but it does not serve to align the women with Peter. Rather, it creates a distinction between them. The women do not move farther away from Jesus, but closer to him.

The women's fearful flight from the tomb in Mark 16:8, however, casts a long shadow over their narrative portrait. The gravity of their perceived disobedience has at times been used to argue that Mark does not intend to portray the women as disciples of Jesus in any way.[11] Yet, even if the final act of the women is one of fearful disobedience, their introduction into the narrative serves as evidence of Mark's intentional portrayal of them as disciples. Mark asserts that the three named women, along with the larger group of anonymous women whom they represent, were both "following" (ἠκολούθουν) and "serving" (διηκόνουν) Jesus (Mark 15:40-41). These particular actions suggest a close narrative connection between the women and Jesus's own specific teaching on the nature of discipleship, in which the themes of both following and serving are essential (i.e., ἀκολουθέω in Mark 8:34-38; διακονέω in Mark 10:42-45).[12]

The women's delayed introduction into the narrated events of the Gospel suggests an attempt not to silence their importance in the narrative but rather to emphasize it. The twelve disciples have abandoned Jesus (Mark 14:50-52; 66-72) and the audience is now introduced to an alternative group of disciples who have been present with Jesus throughout his ministry and will remain with him throughout the climactic events of the narrative. The women's presence at Jesus's crucifixion (Mark 15:40-41), burial (Mark 15:47), and resurrection (Mark 16:1-7) highlights their position not as failed or fallible followers but as faithful witnesses.

Most interpreters note the positive value of the women as witnesses in the final section of the narrative in Mark 15 and the initial portion of Mark 16. Their more negative assessment of the women stems primarily from the culminating events of Mark 16:8, particularly the women's immediate departure from the tomb—"they went out and fled from the tomb, because terror and amazement gripped them"—and their fearful and apparently disobedient silence—"they said nothing to anyone, because they were afraid." The rapid transition from the introduction of the women as essential witnesses to the climactic events of the narrative to their apparent failure seems highly incongruous. Indeed, as R. T. France notes:

---

11. See, e.g., Munro, "Women Disciples," 225-41.

12. For a discussion of Mark's development of these terms, see Kinukawa, *Women and Jesus in Mark*, 96-102. See also Witherington, *Women in the Ministry of Jesus*.

Part Two—Narratives *of* Discipleship

> for Mark to build up so carefully the women's unique role as the first witnesses of the fact of resurrection only to knock it down in his final sentence by insisting on their complete silence seems bizarre. It is one thing to emphasise and exploit paradoxical elements within the story of Jesus' ministry and passion ... but quite another to conclude his gospel with a note which appears to undermine not only his own message but also the received tradition of the church within which he was writing.[13]

An ancient solution to this literary incongruity was to supply a different ending to Mark's Gospel, either after omitting the reference to the women's apparent failure or simply circumventing it with subsequent material.[14] In light of the near scholarly unanimity that the Gospel ends at Mark 16:8, however, a more recent explanation suggests that the note of fear upon which the Gospel ends is an extension of the theme of discipleship failure that is prominent throughout Mark's Gospel.[15] Larry Hurtado offers a helpful summary of this interpretive strategy:

> A number of scholars portray the ending of Mark as a rather sophisticated literary/rhetorical device intended to intrigue, disappoint, frustrate and "trap" the intended Christian readers, drawing them through a sophisticated process into some sort of existential completion of the story, thus compensating for the failures of the disciples in general, and the women of 16:1–8 in particular.[16]

Andrew Lincoln argues that the women's failure in Mark 16:8 gives full rhetorical weight to the preceding note of the promise of restoration in Mark 16:7—"the silence of the women [is] overcome by Jesus' word of promise."[17] In his view, the intent of this ending is to call the audience to

13. France, *Gospel of Mark*, 683.

14. Importantly, however, as Hurtado notes, the earliest readers of Mark's Gospel—Matthew and Luke—explain the women's silence not in terms of disobedience but in terms of restriction (Hurtado, "Women, the Tomb," 441).

15. See, e.g., Aquino and McLemore, "Markan Characterization of Women," 423–24; Cotes, "Women, Silence and Fear," 150–66; D'Angelo, "(Re)Presentations of Women in the Gospels," 138; Danove, "Characterization and Narrative Function," 395–97; Dewey, "Women in the Gospel of Mark," 28–29; Fowler, *Let the Reader Understand*, 243–53; Hester, "Dramatic Inconclusion," 61–86; Juel, *Master of Surprise*, 115–21; Lincoln, "Promise and the Failure," 283–300; Mitchell, *Beyond Fear and Silence*, 66–115; Peterson, "When Is the End Not the End? 151–66; Tolbert, *Sowing the Gospel*, 295–99; Tyson, "Blindness of the Disciples," 261–68.

16. Hurtado, "Women, the Tomb," 437.

17. Lincoln, "Promise and the Failure," 292.

Cruciform Discipleship (Mark 15-16)

review Mark's narrative to understand the interplay between the themes of failure and promised fulfillment. Lincoln argues that this ending will allow the audience to enter into the narrative of the Gospel and determine whether it wants to live out the way of the cross or to mirror both the male and female disciples in their fear and disobedience. In Lincoln's words, "the impact of [this] juxtaposition is encouragement to persevere despite failure and disobedience."[18] Given their own experience and knowledge of the narrative, the audience of Mark's Gospel is meant to reverse the action of the women (as well as that of the other disciples) by living as faithful followers of the crucified Messiah in the temporal divide between Jesus's resurrection and return.

As Hurtado notes, the primary difficulty with this view is that no other ancient text exhibits a suspended or open ending in which the audience is meant not simply to supply a section of missing information but to reverse an aspect of the narrative's ending by supplying *alternative* information.[19] If Mark has intentionally redacted a previous tradition about the discovery of Jesus's resurrection to emphasize the theme of discipleship failure, then he has undermined the veracity of the women's testimony and given little support for his late introduction of them into the narrative. Richard Bauckham's concise evaluation of the theory is constructive: "It is not plausible to read the end of Mark's story of the empty tomb as an ironic device that deconstructs the story's own truth claims."[20] To portray the women as failed disciples neglects the wider contours of their narrative portrayal in Mark 15-16.

The difficulty of the rhetorical device developed in the reading of Lincoln and others is not that it recognizes that Mark ends his Gospel in such a way as to call the audience to enter into a reenactment of the narrative. Mark does intend to transform his audience through the development of the narrative in general and through the dramatic description of Jesus's death

---

18. Ibid., 297.

19. Hurtado, "Women, the Tomb," 437-38. Proponents of the view developed in Lincoln's essay often point to the essential work of J. Lee Magness in showing that open endings existed in the ancient world. Magness, however, never argued for an open ending in which the reader was meant to supply *alternative* information from that developed in the context. In addition, Magness himself argued that the final phrase in Mark 16:8 referred to a temporally constrained silence, not a form of universal failure (*Sense and Absence*, 100).

20. Bauckham, *Gospel Women*, 289. On the function of the women as witnesses in the resurrection narratives, see ibid., 257-310.

Part Two—Narratives *of* Discipleship

and resurrection in particular. The problematic nature of the proposal is its portrayal of the women as negative exemplars who need to be overcome so that the reality of Jesus's cross and resurrection can be known, experienced, and embodied in the community. The call to a form of discipleship that is defined by Mark's Christology is an essential purpose of the narrative. But this discipleship is rooted in the narrative portrayal of the women in Mark 15-16 not detached from it.

The Narrative Witness of the Named Women

The apparent incongruity of the portrayal of the women in Mark 15-16, as well as the problematic nature of some of these recent proposals, has led several scholars to interpret Mark 16:1-8 in a way that maintains a positive assessment of the women.[21] Hurtado has developed a cohesive description of the narrative function of the women as named witnesses of the climactic events of the Gospel. In his conclusion, Hurtado argues:

> Mark 16:1-8 forms a fully satisfactory climactic episode that was designed to thrill and empower intended readers to follow Jesus in mission, through opposition and even their own potentially violent death, confident in an eschatological vindication by resurrection for which Jesus' resurrection was the inspiring model.[22]

The crux of this argument is a more positive reading of Mark 16:8 in which the women apparently flee from the tomb in fearful and disobedient silence, failing to report the message of restoration they received. Although most interpreters have understood Mark's assertion that the women "said nothing to anyone" (οὐδενὶ οὐδὲν εἶπαν) as a blanket statement of their failure, this is not the only way in which the phrase may be understood. It has been pointed out by a number of scholars that there is a close correspondence between the language of Mark 16:8 and 1:44, where Jesus instructs a cured leper not to speak to anyone *except* the priest to whom he was to show himself as a testimony of the healing process (μηδενὶ μηδὲν εἴπῃς ἀλλὰ ὕπαγε σεαυτὸν δεῖξον τῷ ἱερεῖ . . . εἰς μαρτύριον αὐτοῖς).[23] The close

---

21. See esp. Bauckham, *Gospel Women*, 286-95; and Hurtado, "Women, the Tomb," 429-50.

22. Hurtado, "Women, the Tomb," 447.

23. See esp. Bauckham, *Gospel Women*, 289; Catchpole, "Fearful Silence," 3-10; Catchpole, *Resurrection People*, 20-28; Dwyer, *Motif of Wonder*, 191-92; Hurtado, "Women, the Tomb," 438-39; Malbon, "Fallible Followers," 45. Hurtado also notes a

Cruciform Discipleship (Mark 15-16)

correspondence between "they said nothing to anyone" (οὐδενὶ οὐδὲν εἶπαν; Mark 16:8) and "say nothing to anyone" (μηδενὶ μηδὲν εἴπῃς; Mark 1:44) may suggest that the emphasis in Mark 16:8 is on a restricted form of communication and not the women's universal silence.[24] On this reading, the thrust of Mark 16:8 is not that the women remain in perpetual, disobedient silence, but rather that they spoke to no one *except* the disciples to whom they were sent (Mark 16:7).

David Neville contends, however, that the link between Mark 1:44 and 16:8 actually stresses the disobedience of the women. Whereas in Mark 1:44 the double negative (μηδενὶ μηδὲν) emphasizes Jesus's command, the double negative in Mark 16:8 (οὐδενὶ οὐδὲν) emphasizes the women's disobedience. As Neville avers, "In Mark 1:44 the emphatically negative command by Jesus is disobeyed, and in Mark 16:8 the positive command by the young man speaking on Jesus' behalf is emphatically disobeyed!"[25] Although Neville is certainly correct that Mark's use of the double negative is emphatic in each scene, I want to suggest that the importance of the parallel rests not on the category of obedience but on the category of restriction. The leper in Mark 1 proves his disobedience to Jesus by reporting the reality of his restoration beyond the restricted scope of its intended audience (the priest). The women in Mark 16 demonstrate their obedience to Jesus's surrogate by reporting the reality of the resurrection only to the restricted audience to whom they were sent (the disciples). As with the connection between the portraits of Peter at Jesus's trial (Mark 14:54) and the women at Jesus's crucifixion (Mark 15:40), the parallel between Mark 1:44 and 16:8 serves to distinguish the women's action from that of the leper.

That the women's action in speaking to no one (else) is not an act of disobedience is also supported by Mark's use of the term "and" (καί) to introduce both of the initial clauses in Mark 16:8 (καὶ ἐξελθοῦσαι ἔφυγον . . . καὶ οὐδενὶ οὐδὲν εἶπαν). The narrative movement does not stress that their departure or their silence was in *contrast* to the command they received to speak to the disciples, for which a clear adversative—"but" (e.g., δέ or ἀλλά)—would have been more appropriate.[26] Rather, the narrative

---

correspondence with Mark 7:36 in which Jesus commands the disciples to speak to no one (διεστείλατο αὐτοῖς ἵνα μηδενὶ λέγωσιν), where in context "no one" (μηδενί) must refer to "no one *else*" ("Women, the Tomb," 439).

24. Hurtado, "Women, the Tomb," 439; cf. Bayer, *Markus*, 589.

25. Neville, "Creation Reclaimed," 110.

26. See the development of this argument in Evans, *Mark 8:27-16:20*, 539; Gundry, *Mark*, 1010; Hurtado, "Women, the Tomb," 439.

Part Two—Narratives *of* Discipleship

movement suggests simply the consecutive nature of their departure and restricted silence after their reception of the news about Jesus's resurrection and the command to reiterate Jesus's promise to meet the disciples in Galilee (cf. Mark 14:28).

In spite of this more positive proposal that Mark 16:8 refers to a form of restricted communication between the women and the disciples, there are other elements of the narrative which may still require a negative interpretation of Mark's portrayal of the women. One such element is the fact that the women flee from the tomb. And another is the fear that apparently prevents them from speaking. Both the terms "flee" (φεύγω) and "fear" (φοβέω) are frequently associated with earlier sections of Mark's narrative that highlight aspects of discipleship failure.[27] For example, the women's rapid departure from the tomb is often connected with the earlier flight of the disciples in Gethsemane (Mark 14:50)—"all of them abandoned him and fled" (καὶ ἀφέντες αὐτὸν ἔφυγον πάντες; cf. Mark 14:52), with the result that the women's act of fleeing is seen to embody the same dimensions of failure as are highlighted in the disciples' abandonment of Jesus during his arrest. While there is certainly a connection between the narrative of the disciples in Gethsemane and the narrative of the women at the tomb, it seems reasonable to argue that the impact of the connection is again not one of comparison but of contrast. The direction of the disciples' flight is *away* from Jesus because of the reality of his arrest. The direction of the women's flight is *toward* the disciples because of their commission to inform them of the reality of Jesus's resurrection. Bauckham provides a clear assessment of the relationship between the flight of the disciples and the women:

> At first sight it seems plausible that the women's flight parallels that of the men in Gethsemane (14:50, 52), but only so long as we remain at the level of words instead of envisaging the realistic situations Mark depicts. The flight of the men in Gethsemane is a failure to stand by Jesus, a failure to follow him on the way of the cross, through fear of the danger to themselves. But there is no sense in which the women should have remained in the tomb in order to be faithful to Jesus. Their business in the tomb is in any case finished; the young man has told them to go. Their flight can

---

27. See, e.g., Danove, "Characterization and Narrative Function," 390–92; Neville, "Creation Reclaimed," 110–11; Williams, *Other Followers*, 197–98.

hardly be a failure of discipleship, even if their failure to speak is.[28]

The disciples fled from Jesus in contrast to the call of discipleship. The women flee from the tomb in response to a direct command to fulfill the call of discipleship and to bring a message of restoration to those disciples who abandoned Jesus.

The women's fearful silence is also tied to negative connotations associated with the language of fear (φοβέω) in earlier sections of Mark's narrative (e.g., Mark 4:41; 5:15, 36; 6:20, 50; 9:32; 10:32; 11:18, 32; 12:12; cf. 9:6).[29] That is, one might argue that even if the women's silence was in fact restricted, their fear still represents an example of discipleship failure. As with our earlier discussion of the language of fear in the narrative of the bleeding woman (Mark 5:25–34), the most relevant example, given the frequent comparisons between the twelve disciples and these named women, is the narrative in Mark 4 in which the disciples' lack of faith during the storm on the sea is closely connected with their fear (Mark 4:37–41).[30] In the context of Mark 4, the disciples wake Jesus and question his concern for them in the midst of the storm. Jesus responds by rebuking them, questioning their lack of faith. The specific note of the disciples' fear in Mark 4:41 (ἐφοβήθησαν φόβον μέγαν), however, does not relate back to Jesus's rebuke but is rather a description of the disciples' response to Jesus's ability to calm the storm.[31] In the immediate context of Mark 4 the disciples' fear is not an example of their failure but a description of their response to a divine disclosure. It is this aspect of the disciples' narrative that is paralleled in the women's experience.

The women have encountered an angelic figure, and their experience is marked by the normal pattern of fearful response (cf. Judg 6:22–23; Dan 8:17; 10:7, 12; Luke 2:9–10; Rev 1:17).[32] The entirety of Mark 16:8 reflects the

28. Bauckham, *Gospel Women*, 288.

29. Danove, "Characterization and Narrative Function," 391-92; cf. Lincoln, "Promise and the Failure," 286-87; Moloney, *Gospel of Mark*, 348-49.

30. Danove, "Characterization and Narrative Function," 391-92.

31. So Bauckham, *Gospel Women*, 290; cf. Collins, *Mark*, 800; Dwyer, *Motif of Wonder*, 109-11; Marcus, *Mark*, 1:334.

32. Marcus, *Mark*, 2:1085; cf. Williams, "Narrative Space," 277-80. On the notion that the "young man" (νεανίσκος) in Mark 16:5 is in fact an angelic figure (ἄγγελος), see Boring, *Mark*, 444-48; Collins, *Mark*, 795-96; Dwyer, *Motif of Wonder*, 185-93. On the potential (though unlikely) relationship with the "young man" (νεανίσκος) in Mark 14:51-52, see Marcus, *Mark*, 2:1124-25.

Part Two—Narratives *of* Discipleship

women's response to their discovery of Jesus's absence from the tomb and the dramatic nature of the message of his resurrection.[33] The reality of their numinous experience results in a multiplicity of emotional responses— "they were alarmed" (ἐξεθαμβήθησαν; Mark 16:5), "terror and amazement gripped them" (εἶχεν . . . αὐτὰς τρόμος καὶ ἔκστασις; Mark 16:8), and "they were afraid" (ἐφοβοῦντο; Mark 16:8). Mark does not describe these emotional responses as something that inhibits or paralyzes the women but as the catalyst for their departure from the tomb. In the midst of this powerful experience, the women flee the scene to fulfill the specific commission that they had received. The women's fear represents not their failure or misunderstanding but rather their recognition of the divine drama unfolding before them.[34]

Throughout the narrative of Mark 15-16 these women function as faithful observers of the climactic events of the Gospel—the crucifixion, burial, and resurrection of Jesus. Given this more positive assessment of the women's role in this section of Mark's narrative, it seems reasonable to suggest an amendment to the otherwise measured and helpful reading of the Markan characters developed in the influential work of Elizabeth Struthers Malbon. In her 1983 article "Fallible Followers," Malbon argued that the female characters in Mark's narrative could be understood along a spectrum of discipleship that was more extensively developed in the portrait of Jesus's male disciples.[35] In a slight emendation to her argument, Malbon then argued in her 1994 essay on the minor characters in Mark's narrative that the narrated stories of women prior to Mark 15:40—with the clear exception of Herodias and her daughter (Mark 6:14-29)—were all better characterized as *exemplars* of faithful and active discipleship.[36] Yet, in light of her understanding of the phrase "from a distance" (Mark 15:40) and her perception of the women's failed report (Mark 16:8), Malbon continued to assert that the women who appear in Mark 15-16 were fallible followers, demonstrating the same potential for both success and failure portrayed in Mark's portrait of the twelve disciples.[37]

---

33. Cf. Collins, *Mark*, 799-800; Hurtado, "Women, the Tomb," 439-40.

34. Contra Miller, *Women in Mark's Gospel*, 187.

35. Malbon, "Fallible Followers," 32-35.

36. Malbon, "Minor Characters," 69n3.

37. Ibid., 69, 72. This paradigm is largely maintained in Miller, *Women in Mark's Gospel*.

Cruciform Discipleship (Mark 15-16)

The preceding argument, however, suggests Mark may not be focusing on fallibility at all. The late appearance of the women in the narrative and their presence during its climactic events imply a specific contrast with the male disciples who have played a prominent role in the narrative but have abandoned Jesus at this crucial stage. The women in Mark 15-16 maintain the same positive portrayal of discipleship consistently developed in the previous narratives of female characters (i.e., Mark 1:29-31; 5:25-34; 7:24-30; 12:41-44; 14:3-9). Again, the intent of this argument is not to suggest an oversimplified portrait of the male disciples as complete failures or the women as free from the reality of the difficulty of discipleship, but to suggest with Hurtado that the women in Mark 15-16 have a clear narrative function as faithful witnesses.[38] Or, to build on the language of Malbon, the women who witness Jesus's crucifixion, burial, and resurrection are faithful exemplars of Markan discipleship.

The Narrative Discipleship of the Named Women

After developing an overtly positive portrait of the women in Mark 15-16, Hurtado returns to the question of the abruptness of the ending of Mark's Gospel. He contends that the absence of developed resurrection appearances—though not the absence of the resurrection itself (cf. Mark 16:7)—is best explained by Mark's emphasis on the central importance of the cross in the development of his Christology. Hurtado argues:

> The Markan narrative stresses that the crucifixion of Jesus is not simply overcome in his resurrection, as an ordeal that could now be regarded as a temporary setback like the trials of a Greek hero. Instead, the point is that the risen Jesus remains the same Jesus who was crucified (16:6), and that the events of death, burial and resurrection are together essential in mutually interpreting one another.[39]

Hurtado's emphasis on the importance of the cross for the development of Mark's Christology resonates with his argument in an earlier essay that this emphasis on the cross is in fact the paradigm of Christian discipleship:

---

38. Hurtado, "Women, the Tomb," 427-49.
39. Ibid., 445.

Part Two—Narratives *of* Discipleship

Mark's christological emphasis falls more on the cross as the disclosure of the meaning of Jesus, which is why an accurate understanding of Jesus is withheld from all human characters in Mark's Gospel until the crucifixion. This cross-emphasis in Mark's view of Jesus' mission coheres with his emphasis on Jesus' crucifixion as the paradigm of faithful discipleship. The shortcomings of the Twelve and the positive example of Jesus together form major components in Mark's literary and didactic plan—the Twelve functioning as warning examples of the dangers that readers must avoid and Jesus' example functioning to show what faithful discipleship looks like. Discipleship, Mark emphasizes, means *following* Jesus, with the story of Jesus serving as the paradigm.[40]

Hurtado's summaries are a constructive explanation of the close connection in Mark's narrative between Christology and discipleship. What is missing from both, however, is the women of Mark 15–16. In fact, Hurtado stresses that one of the benefits of a positive reading of Mark 16:8 is that it allows "these women to step back quickly out of the public limelight (joining the other disciples, who have been on the sidelines all through the crucifixion-resurrection narratives)."[41] Hurtado is certainly right to stress the christological and cross-shaped emphasis of Mark's narrative. But his sidelining of the women at the end of his argument fails to maintain his discussion of their positive narrative function. The fact that their presence with Jesus is narrated only in connection with the passion and resurrection narratives suggests both their close identification with those events and their contrast with the other disciples who are no longer present. Their rapid departure from the narrative is not an act of stepping back but of stepping forward as bearers of the message of restoration. To put it another way, the women's role in the narrative is conditioned by the reality of Jesus's crucifixion, death, and resurrection. They are the essential narrative representatives of these central events in the Gospel. In this way the women function as exemplars of discipleship, providing a "narrative exclamation point" for Mark's description of the close relationship between Christology and discipleship.[42] Mark portrays the women as narrative exemplars of a form of faithful discipleship that reflects the paradigm established in Jesus by positioning them as participants in the climactic events of the Gospel.

40. Hurtado, "Following Jesus," 25 (emphasis original).
41. Hurtado, "Women, the Tomb," 443.
42. On Mark's use of "narrative punctuation," see Malbon, "Minor Characters," 72–73.

Cruciform Discipleship (Mark 15–16)

The idea that Markan discipleship is defined by the paradigm created in Jesus's life, death, and resurrection develops from the close association that Mark establishes between Jesus's passion–resurrection predictions and the nature of discipleship. The three passion–resurrection predictions in Mark's Gospel exhibit a rhetorical pattern that connects Jesus's proclamations with an instance of discipleship failure and a subsequent call to a reimagined form of discipleship (Mark 8:31–38; 9:30–37; 10:32–45). Each prediction reveals content about Jesus's ministry and connects it with the definition of discipleship. Given the implicitly exhortative nature of this material, Michael Gorman argues that we should refer to each section "not merely as a 'passion prediction' but as a 'passion prediction-summons,' meaning a call to passion-shaped discipleship, or, in a word, cruciformity."[43] Gorman uses this language of "cruciformity" to describe the way in which Christ's own cross-shaped narrative is paradigmatic for the life of Christ's followers.[44] Gorman's specific emphasis on the cross does not diminish the importance of the resurrection but rather emphasizes the revelatory and creative characteristics of the cross itself. It both defines the nature of Christ's identity and creates the community in which this cruciform paradigm is expressed.[45] What develops at these crucial points in Mark's narrative is a series of implicit exhortations that positions the self-sacrificial character of Jesus's ministry as the essential paradigm for the lives of his followers.

Perhaps the most paradigmatic of these summonses is developed in Mark 8:34: "If anyone wants to follow (ἀκολουθεῖν) me they must deny themselves and take up their cross and follow (ἀκολουθείτω) me." There is a clear association here between Jesus's passion and the life of discipleship—"to follow Christ in the way of the cross is more akin to participating in the reality or life or story of God . . . than to following someone at a distance or even imitating a master."[46] Indeed, as Susan Miller notes, the "death and resurrection of Jesus may only be understood by those who follow the way of the cross."[47] Given the emphasis on the language of following in Mark 8:34, Mark's assertion that the women were "following" (ἠκολούθουν) Jesus

---

43. Gorman, *Death of the Messiah*, 84.

44. On the language of cruciformity, see esp. Gorman, *Cruciformity*; and Gorman, *Inhabiting the Cruciform God*.

45. Gorman, *Death of the Messiah*, 34–36.

46. Ibid., 36.

47. Miller, *Women in Mark's Gospel*, 184.

Part Two—Narratives *of* Discipleship

(Mark 15:41) likely harks back to this exhortation and positions them as disciples within the narrative. Discipleship means *following* Jesus in the way of the cross. These women are the only characters that Mark portrays as following Jesus in the course of the climactic events of the narrative. Their persistent narrative presence demonstrates their commitment to the cruciform nature of Jesus's gospel.

The final passion–resurrection prediction (Mark 10:32–45) reflects this same christological focus in its summons to the disciples to redefine their ideals about greatness so that they can participate in the same form of service that Jesus himself embodies. To lean again on the language of Gorman, Jesus's act of service is both unique and paradigmatic.[48] His death and resurrection create a new reality in which disciples are called to live in a way that reflects the same pattern of service. As with the narrative of Simon's mother-in-law (Mark 1:29–31), Mark's use of the language of service connects his portrayal of Jesus—"For even the Son of Man did not come to be served (διακονηθῆναι), but to serve (διακονῆσαι), and to give his life as a ransom for many" (Mark 10:45)—with that of the named women— "who were following and serving (διηκόνουν) Jesus when he was in Galilee" (Mark 15:41). The only human agents to whom this key discipleship term is attributed, apart from Jesus, are women (Mark 1:29; 15:40–41). The named women are here again introduced into the narrative as positive exemplars of a form of discipleship that evokes Jesus's earlier teaching. Both these specific linguistic connections and the women's narrative position as participants in the story of Jesus's passion and resurrection suggest their function as narrative examples of Mark's wider portrait of cruciform discipleship.

Gorman develops the language of cruciformity and cruciform discipleship particularly with reference to the Pauline epistles. He argues that Paul's statements about life in Christ establish Christ as the paradigm for Christian existence. Since Christ is the crucified one (1 Cor 1:23; cf. Mark 16:6), participation in the new covenant community he inaugurates through his death and resurrection means participation in that same cross-shaped existence. The pattern of discipleship that Paul develops is that of an imitation, embodiment, and participation in the narrative of Jesus. In his work *The Death of the Messiah and the Birth of the New Covenant*, Gorman establishes the presence of this cruciform pattern throughout the witness of the wider New Testament, including the way it develops in Mark's Gospel.[49]

48. Gorman, *Death of the Messiah*, 117.
49. Ibid., esp. 33–36, 81–94, 106–11, 114–27.

Cruciform Discipleship (Mark 15-16)

Gorman shows that Mark, like Paul, develops his understanding of discipleship in light of the inherent exhortations developed in Jesus's predictions of his death and resurrection.[50] Mark's narrative portrays Jesus as the ultimate paradigm of discipleship and calls its audience to live in a way that reflects Jesus's cruciform identity.

The unique introduction of the women into Mark's narrative both as witnesses to Jesus's crucifixion and burial and as recipients of the news of his resurrection allows them to function as narrative representations of this type of cruciform discipleship. Mark portrays the women as the only ones who faithfully follow Jesus in the midst of his suffering, death, and resurrection. To coordinate the narrative of Mark with the rhetoric of Paul we can suggest that Paul's theological emphasis on the theme of participation in Christ—being "in Christ"—is represented in Mark's Gospel by these named women whose narrative function is to establish, verify, and proclaim the consequence of the climactic events of the Gospel. The women are narrative embodiments of the reality of cruciform discipleship.

CONCLUSION

The purpose of this chapter was to describe the way in which Mark's narrative portrayal of the named women in the story of Jesus's passion and resurrection (Mark 15:40–41, 47; 16:1–8) impacts his wider definition of discipleship. I argued that Mark's intentional introduction of these named women in the climactic scenes of the Gospel establishes them as narrative representatives of *cruciform discipleship*. Although these named women are often seen to move along the same trajectory of faithfulness and failure that defines Mark's portrayal of the twelve disciples, their narrative function in the Gospel can be interpreted more positively as a coherent demonstration of Markan discipleship. The women's late introduction into the narrated story creates a direct association between them and the climactic events of the narrative—Jesus's crucifixion, burial, and resurrection. Their close association with these events establishes their role in the narrative as faithful witnesses and exemplars of those who follow Jesus on the way of the cross. This portrait of the women reflects the cruciform discipleship that Mark emphasizes throughout the Gospel. Mark depicts the life of discipleship as conformity to the cruciform existence of Jesus. The named women in Mark 15–16 embody a narrative presentation of the cruciform discipleship

50. Ibid., 130–31.

Part Two—Narratives *of* Discipleship

that demonstrates the way in which the cross forces Mark to reimagine the nature of the new covenant community inaugurated in God's in-breaking kingdom.

Conclusion

NARRATIVE DISCIPLESHIP—A SYNTHESIS

MARK'S GOSPEL COMPELS ITS audience toward enacted participation in God's kingdom. The Gospel's theological narrative of Jesus's life, death, and resurrection moves toward an aretegenic end. The intent of Mark's narrative is to create an embodied form of virtue in which those transformed by the message of God's in-breaking kingdom become active participants in the renewal of creation and the reordering of humanity in the image of Christ. This embodied virtue defines the content and shape of Markan discipleship. The form of discipleship toward which Mark's narrative directs its audience is a dynamic embodiment of the transformative reality of God's kingdom that is marked by faithful allegiance to the crucified and resurrected Jesus.

Mark achieves this aretegenic goal through the literary form of the Gospel. As a unified narrative the Gospel not only provides biographical and scriptural insight into the identity of Jesus, it functions as a mirror in which the audience can identify its own reflection and determine whether the contours of its shape coordinate with the image of Jesus that the narrative casts. This aretegenic mirror is illuminated for the audience by Mark's creative description of Jesus's ministry and passion and his intentional portrayal (characterization) of those who engage with Jesus (characters). Mark's Gospel moves toward its aretegenic end through the narrative intersection of the portrayal of Jesus and his interaction with other characters. The audience learns to embody the discipleship toward which the Gospel aims by reflecting and enacting the essential virtues (characteristics) that

Conclusion

Mark portrays in Jesus's embodiment of God's kingdom and the way in which the kingdom impacts upon those with whom Jesus interacts.

This literary framework is what we have described as *narrative discipleship*. Narrative discipleship refers to the composite set of actions and attributes associated with the identity of Jesus and derived from the cruciform shape of his life and ministry which Mark portrays in the Gospel as essential for those who desire to participate in the reality of God's in-breaking kingdom. The portrait of narrative discipleship that Mark creates is extensive. It encompasses both major characters such as the twelve disciples who feature extensively throughout the narrative and minor characters such as the women whose narrative presence is more limited. The contribution of these distinct groups to Mark's portrait of narrative discipleship demonstrates that the significance of characters in the narrative is determined not by the frequency with which they appear but rather by the thematic contribution of their contextual engagement with Jesus. The limited narrative presence of the women does not diminish their contribution to Mark's aretegenic agenda. In contrast, the primary thesis that I have developed is that Mark's intentional portrayal of eight women creates a trajectory of faithfulness that extends the boundaries of his portrait of narrative discipleship.

The narratives of these eight women—Simon's mother-in-law (Mark 1:29–31), the bleeding woman (Mark 5:25–34), the Syrophoenician woman (Mark 7:24–30), the poor widow (Mark 12:41–44), the woman who anoints Jesus (Mark 14:3–9), and the three named women in the passion narrative (Mark 15:40–41, 47; 16:1–8)—reflect the way in which God's kingdom renews creation and redefines humanity in the image of Christ. When linked together their narratives create a composite portrayal that emphasizes four essential characteristics of Markan discipleship—restored life, kingdom speech, sacrificial action, and cruciformity. While these four characteristics do not represent the sum total of Mark's portrait of discipleship, they offer a constructive frame within which Mark's audience may discern the impact of God's kingdom and reflect upon what it means to demonstrate faithful allegiance to the crucified and resurrected Jesus.

The narrative discipleship developed in the portraits of these eight women is crucially connected to Mark's wider narrative of the way in which God's kingdom breaks into the world in the life, death, and resurrection of Jesus. The four essential characteristics of discipleship which their narratives emphasize demonstrate key realities that define both the kingdom and those who seek to participate in it. God's kingdom is an act of re-creation.

Conclusion

The healing that Simon's mother-in-law and the bleeding woman receive from Jesus is not mere physical restoration. The narrative portrayal of their healing points outward toward the transformed life that defines the restorative dimension of God's kingdom. The dramatic healings of these women function as narrative illustrations of God's comprehensive restoration. Like these women, those who encounter God's kingdom are called to participate in its restored reality.

God's kingdom brings about the transformation of cultural and social structures. Within the boundaries of restoration that God's kingdom creates there exists a call to proclaim this transformative reality. As the Syrophoenician woman seeks the restoration of her daughter, Mark positions her as one with the capacity to speak Jesus's λόγος. The kingdom-oriented focus of the woman's engagement with Jesus in spite of her status as a cultural outsider emphasizes her appropriate recognition of the inclusive reality of God's kingdom. Like this woman, those who encounter God's kingdom are called to speak its message of transformed inclusion.

God's kingdom is defined by the paradoxical narrative of Jesus. Mark's portrayal of Jesus demonstrates that the restorative reality of the kingdom is conditioned not by victory but sacrifice. The portraits of the poor widow and the woman who anoints Jesus serve as narrative expressions of the comprehensive sacrifice that Jesus embodies in his own ministry. The holistic nature of the sacrifice that each woman makes reiterates Jesus's call to forsake everything to follow him. Like these women, those who encounter God's kingdom are called to embody its paradoxical reality in sacrificial action.

God's kingdom is defined by the crucifixion and resurrection of Jesus. Mark's integrated portrayal of these events emphasizes the vindication of the crucified Jesus as the resurrected king. Mark's portrayal of the named women who witness Jesus's crucifixion, burial, and resurrection does not culminate in an act of discipleship failure, but rather creates a close narrative connection between the message of the crucified and resurrected one and the identity of those who seek to follow him. Like these women, those who encounter God's kingdom are called to form their lives on the pattern of the crucified and resurrected Jesus.

Conclusion

NARRATIVE DISCIPLESHIP—A SUMMONS

Mark's narrative portrait of God's in-breaking kingdom is not neutral. Mark's Gospel is itself a theological act. It is a piece of narrative communication with a specific aretegenic aim. Our engagement with Mark's narrative as contemporary interpreters involves engagement with historical information about the life and ministry of Jesus and requires interaction with the wider canonical portrait of Jesus's identity and mission. Yet, while historical context and canonical cohesion are essential dimensions of the interpretive process, neither captures the specific aim of Mark's Gospel as narrative. As narrative Mark's Gospel is an act of theological communication intended to transform its audience. The narrative in-breaking of God's kingdom in the life, death, and resurrection of Jesus compels the audience of the Gospel to live in a new way—to participate in the narrative of the kingdom as faithful disciples. Mark creates a portrait of *narrative discipleship* as a means to encourage his audience toward *embodied discipleship*.

Mark's narrative portrayal of the eight women examined in the present volume constitutes a key literary device to compel the audience toward this vision of embodied discipleship. The collective portrait that the narratives of these women create represents a specific expression of Markan discipleship. Mark's intentional portrayal of the characteristics of restored life, kingdom speech, sacrificial action, and cruciformity creates a broad framework for faithful allegiance to Jesus. The contribution of a narrative analysis of Mark's portrayal of these women is its identification of thematic boundaries that can shape the formation of contemporary disciples who desire to participate in the narrative of God's in-breaking kingdom.

Embodied participation in God's kingdom requires a rejection of distinctly human claims about the nature of reality. Mark's narrative presentation of Jesus's incarnation, death, and resurrection demonstrate that reality is defined only by God's action. God's act of restoration in Jesus brings about the renewal and reshaping of the created order. Discipleship in this context requires an equally reordered shaping of perspective and values. The identity of the disciple cannot be rooted in the created order because this is precisely the realm that God transforms. Our distinct cultural, economic, and social narratives need to be reshaped in light of this transformative act of re-creation. In narrating the story of Jesus's embodiment of God's kingdom in his incarnation and the vindication of his kingship in his death and resurrection, Mark calls his audience to pattern their lives according to the same narrative. The identity and action of disciples must be

Conclusion

rooted in a faithful allegiance to the crucified king who himself embodies the kingdom.

This form of faithful allegiance impacts the entirety of human existence. Mark's narrative of discipleship is not one that is defined by compartmentalization. In contrast, the portrait of discipleship created by the composite portrayal of the women is one of cohesion. For this reason, participation in God's kingdom requires not only an inversion of human systems but a conversion of the human imagination. To lean on the language of Kevin Vanhoozer, the imagination is a "formative power" that, when conditioned by the scriptural narrative, enables disciples to embody God's kingdom in a way that integrates their speech, action, and existence.[1] This integrated portrait of embodied discipleship represents the aretegenic aim of Mark's narrative. The identity and action of disciples must be rooted in a holistic re-imagination of their existence as inhabitants of God's kingdom.

---

1. See Vanhoozer, *Pictures at a Theological Exhibition*, 23–27.

Bibliography

Aernie, Jeffrey W. "Cruciform Discipleship: The Narrative Function of the Women in Mark 15–16." *JBL* 135 (2016) 779–97.
Alonso, Pablo. *The Woman Who Changed Jesus: Crossing Boundaries in Mk 7,24–30*. BTS 11. Leuven: Peeters, 2011.
Aquino, Frederick D., and A. Brian McLemore. "Markan Characterization of Women." In *Essays on Women in Earliest Christianity*, edited by Carroll D. Osburn, 393–424. Eugene, OR: Wipf & Stock, 1993.
Aune, David E. "Magic in Early Christianity." *ANRW* 2.32.2 (1980) 1507–57.
Barton, Stephen C. "Mark as Narrative: The Story of the Anointing Woman (Mk 14:3–9)." *ExpTim* 102 (1991) 230–34.
Bates, Matthew W. *Salvation by Allegiance Alone: Rethinking Faith, Works, and the Gospel of Jesus the King*. Grand Rapids: Baker Academic, 2017.
Bauckham, Richard. *Gospel Women: Studies of the Named Women in the Gospels*. Grand Rapids: Eerdmans, 2002.
Bayer, Hans F. *Das Evangelium des Markus*. Historisch Theologische Auslegung. Wuppertal: Brockhaus, 2008.
———. *A Theology of Mark: The Dynamic between Christianity and Authentic Discipleship*. Explorations in Biblical Theology. Phillipsburg: P&R, 2012.
Beavis, Mary Ann. *Mark*. Paideia. Grand Rapids: Baker Academic, 2011.
———. "Women as Models of Faith in Mark." *BTB* 18 (1988) 3–9.
Bengston, Hermann. "Syrien in der hellenistischen Zeit." In *Der Hellenismus und der Aufstieg Roms*, edited by Pierre Grimal, 244–54. Die Mittelmeerwelt im Altertum 2. Frankfurt: Fischer, 1965.
Bennema, Cornelis. *A Theory of Character in New Testament Narrative*. Minneapolis: Fortress, 2014.
Best, Ernest. *Following Jesus: Discipleship in the Gospel of Mark*. JSNTSup 4. Sheffield: JSOT, 1981.
Betsworth, Sharon. *The Reign of God Is Such as These: A Socio-Literary Analysis of Daughters in the Gospel of Mark*. LNTS 422. London: T. & T. Clark, 2010.
Black, C. Clifton. *The Disciples according to Mark: Markan Redaction in Current Debate*. 2nd ed. Grand Rapids: Eerdmans, 2012.
———. *Mark*. ANTC. Nashville: Abingdon, 2011.
Bolt, Peter. "Mark 13: An Apocalyptic Precursor to the Passion Narrative." *RTR* 54 (1995) 10–32.
Boring, M. Eugene. *Mark: A Commentary*. NTL. Louisville: Westminster John Knox, 2006.

Bibliography

———. "Markan Christology: God-Language for Jesus?" *NTS* 45 (1999) 451–71.
Broadhead, Edwin. *Naming Jesus: Titular Christology in the Gospel of Mark*. JSNTSup 175. Sheffield: Sheffield Academic, 1992.
———. *Prophet, Son, Messiah: Narrative Form and Function in Mark 14–16*. JSNTSup 97. Sheffield: JSOT, 1994.
Burer, Michael H. "Narrative Genre: Studying the Story." In *Interpreting the New Testament Text: Introduction to the Art and Science of Exegesis*, edited by Darrell L. Bock and Buist M. Fanning, 197–219. Wheaton: Crossway, 2006.
Burnett, Fred W. "Characterization and Reader Construction of Characters in the Gospels." *Semeia* 63 (1993) 3–28.
Cadwallader, Alan H. *Beyond the Word of a Woman: Recovering the Bodies of the Syrophoenician Women*. Adelaide: ATF, 2008.
Calvin, John. *Commentary on a Harmony of the Evangelists*. 3 vols. Edinburgh: Calvin Translation Society, 1866.
Camery-Hoggatt, Jerry. *Irony in Mark's Gospel: Text and Subtext*. SNTSMS 72. Cambridge: Cambridge University Press, 1992.
Catchpole, David. "The Fearful Silence of the Women at the Tomb: A Study in Markan Theology." *JTSA* 18 (1977) 3–10.
———. *Resurrection People: Studies in the Resurrection Narratives of the Gospels*. Sarum Theological Lectures. London: Darton, Longman, & Todd, 2000.
Charry, Ellen T. *By the Renewing of Your Minds: The Pastoral Function of Christian Doctrine*. Oxford: Oxford University Press, 1999.
Chatman, Seymour. *Story and Discourse: Narrative Structure in Fiction and Film*. Ithaca, NY: Cornell University Press, 1978.
Clarke, Andrew D. *A Pauline Theology of Church Leadership*. LNTS 362. London: T. & T. Clark, 2008.
Cohen, Shaye. "Menstruants and the Sacred." In *Women's History and Ancient History*, edited by Sarah B. Pomeroy, 273–99. Chapel Hill: University of North Carolina Press, 1991.
Collins, Adela Yarbo. *Mark*. Hermeneia. Minneapolis: Fortress, 2007.
Cotes, Mary. "Women, Silence and Fear (Mark 16:8)." In *Women in the Biblical Tradition*, edited by George J. Brooke, 150–66. Studies in Women and Religion 31. Lewiston, NY: Mellen, 1992.
D'Angelo, Mary Rose. "Gender and Power in the Gospel of Mark: Jairus' Daughter and the Woman with the Flow of Blood." In *Miracles in Jewish and Christian Antiquity: Imagining Truth*, edited by John C. Cavandini, 83–109. Notre Dame Studies in Theology 3. Notre Dame: University of Notre Dame Press, 1999.
———. "(Re)Presentations of Women in the Gospels: John and Mark." In *Women and Christian Origins*, edited by Ross Shepard Kraemer and Mary Rose D'Angelo, 137–45. Oxford: Oxford University Press, 1999.
Danove, Paul L. "The Characterization and Narrative Function of the Women at the Tomb (Mark 15,40–41.47; 16,1–8)." *Bib* 77 (1996) 375–97.
———. *The Rhetoric of Characterization of God, Jesus, and Jesus' Disciples in the Gospel of Mark*. JSNTSup 290. London: T. & T. Clark, 2005.
Davidsen, Ole. *The Narrative Jesus: A Semiotic Reading of Mark's Gospel*. Aarhus: Aarhus University Press, 1993.
Dewey, Joanna. "Jesus' Healings of Women: Conformity and Nonconformity to Dominant Cultural Values as Clues for Historical Reconstruction." *BTB* 24 (1994) 122–31.

Bibliography

———. "Women in the Gospel of Mark." *WW* 26 (2006) 22–29.
Dibelius, Martin. *From Tradition to Gospel*. Translated by B. L. Woolf. London: Nicholson & Waton, 1934.
DiCicco, Mario. "'What Can One Give in Exchange for One's Life?' A Narrative-Critical Study of the Widow and Her Offering, Mark 12:41–44." *CurTM* 25 (1998) 441–49.
Donahue, John R., and Daniel J. Harrington. *The Gospel of Mark*. SP 2. Collegeville, MN: Liturgical, 2002.
Driggers, Ira Brent. *Following God through Mark: Theological Tension in the Second Gospel*. Louisville: Westminster John Knox, 2007.
Dwyer, Timothy. *The Motif of Wonder in the Gospel of Mark*. JSNTSup 128. Sheffield: Sheffield Academic, 1996.
Edwards, James R. *The Gospel according to Mark*. Pillar New Testament Commentary. Grand Rapids: Eerdmans, 2002.
Ernst, Josef. *Das Evangelium nach Markus*. RNT. Regensburg: Pustet, 1981.
Evans, Craig A. *Mark 8:27–16:20*. WBC 34B. Nashville: Thomas Nelson, 2001.
Ewen, Yosef. *Character in Narrative*. Tel Aviv: Sifriyat Hapoalim, 1980.
———. "The Theory of Character in Narrative Fiction." *Hasifrut* 3 (1971) 1–30.
Fander, Monika. *Die Stellung der Frau im Markusevangelium: Unter besonderer Berücksichtigung kultur- und religionsgeschichtlicher Hintergründe*. Münsteraner Theologische Abhandlungen 8. Altenberge: Telos, 1989.
Fonrobert, Charlotte. "The Woman with a Blood-Flow (Mark 5:24–34) Revisited: Menstrual Laws and Jewish Culture in Christian Feminist Hermeneutics." In *Early Christian Interpretation of the Scriptures of Israel: Investigations and Proposals*, edited by Craig A. Evans and James A Sanders, 121–40. JSNTSup 148. SSEJC 5. Sheffield: Sheffield Academic, 1997.
Forster, E. M. *Aspects of the Novel*. New York: Harcourt, Brace, & Co., 1927.
Fowler, Robert M. *Let the Reader Understand: Reader-Response Criticism and the Gospel of Mark*. Minneapolis: Fortress, 1991.
France, R. T. *The Gospel of Mark*. NIGTC. Grand Rapids: Eerdmans, 2002.
Garland, David E. *A Theology of Mark's Gospel: Good News about Jesus the Messiah, the Son of God*. Biblical Theology of the New Testament. Grand Rapids: Zondervan, 2015.
Getty-Sullivan, Mary Ann. *Women in the New Testament*. Collegeville, MN: Liturgical, 2001.
Gorman, Michael J. *Cruciformity: Paul's Narrative Spirituality of the Cross*. Grand Rapids: Eerdmans, 2001
———. *The Death of the Messiah and the Birth of the New Covenant: A (Not So) New Model of the Atonement*. Eugene, OR: Cascade, 2014.
———. *Inhabiting the Cruciform God: Kenosis, Justification, and Theosis in Paul's Narrative Soteriology*. Grand Rapids: Eerdmans, 2009.
Grassi, Joseph A. "The Secret Heroine of Mark's Drama." *BTB* 18 (1988) 10–15.
Guelich, Robert A. *Mark 1–8:26*. WBC 34A. Dallas: Word, 1989.
Gundry, Robert. *Mark: A Commentary on His Apology for the Cross*. Grand Rapids: Eerdmans, 1993.
Haber, Susan. "A Woman's Touch: Feminist Encounters with the Hemorrhaging Woman in Mark 5:24–34." *JSNT* 26 (2003) 171–92.
Hays, Richard B. *The Conversion of the Imagination: Paul as Interpreter of Israel's Scripture*. Grand Rapids: Eerdmans, 2005.

Bibliography

———. *The Moral Vision of the New Testament: A Contemporary Introduction to New Testament Ethics.* San Francisco: HarperCollins, 1996.
Henderson, Suzanne Watts. *Christology and Discipleship in the Gospel of Mark.* SNTSMS 135. Cambridge: Cambridge University Press, 2006.
Hester, David. "Dramatic Inconclusion: Irony and the Narrative Rhetoric of the Ending of Mark." *JSNT* 57 (1995) 61–86.
Hooker, Morna D. *The Gospel according to St Mark.* BNTC. London: A&C Black, 1991.
Hurtado, Larry W. "Following Jesus in the Gospel of Mark—and Beyond." In *Patterns of Discipleship in the New Testament,* edited by Richard N. Longenecker, 9–29. Grand Rapids: Eerdmans, 1996.
———. *Mark.* NIBCNT 2. Peabody, MA: Hendrickson, 1983.
———. "The Women, the Tomb, and the Climax of Mark." In *A Wandering Galilean: Essays in Honour of Seán Freyne,* edited by Zuleika Rodgers, with Margaret Daly-Denton and Anne Fitzpatrick McKinley, 427–50. Journal for the Study of Judaism in the Persian, Hellenistic, and Roman Periods Supplement Series 132. Leiden: Brill, 2009.
Iverson, Kelly R. *Gentiles in the Gospel of Mark: 'Even the Dogs Under the Table Eat the Children's Crumbs'.* LNTS 339. London: T. & T. Clark, 2007.
Iverson, Kelly R., and Christopher W. Skinner, eds. *Mark as Story: Retrospect and Prospect.* RBS 65. Atlanta: Society of Biblical Literature, 2011.
Juel, Donald. *A Master of Surprise: Mark Interpreted.* Minneapolis: Fortress, 1994.
Kähler, Martin. *The So-Called Historical Jesus and the Historic, Biblical Christ.* Translated by C. E. Braaten. Philadelphia: Fortress, 1964.
Kelhoffer, James A. "A Tale of Two Markan Characterizations: The Exemplary Woman Who Anointed Jesus' Body for Burial (14:3–9) and the Silent Trio Who Fled the Empty Tomb (Mark 16:1–8)." In *Women and Gender in Ancient Religions: Interdisciplinary Approaches,* edited by Stephen P. Ahearne-Kroll, Paul A. Holloway, and James A. Kelhoffer, 85–98. WUNT 1/263. Tübingen: Mohr Siebeck, 2010.
Kingsbury, Jack Dean. *The Christology of Mark's Gospel.* Philadelphia: Fortress, 1983.
Kinukawa, Hisako. *Women and Jesus in Mark: A Japanese Feminist Perspective, Bible and Liberation.* Mayknoll, NY: Orbis, 1994.
Krause, Deborah. "Simon Peter's Mother-in-Law—Disciple or Domestic Servant? Feminist Biblical Hermeneutics and the Interpretation of Mark 1.29–31." In *A Feminist Companion to Mark,* edited by Amy-Jill Levine with Marianne Blickenstaff, 37–53. Sheffield: Sheffield Academic, 2001.
Lane, William L. *The Gospel according to Mark.* NICNT. Grand Rapids: Eerdmans, 1974.
Lincoln, Andrew T. "The Promise and the Failure." *JBL* 108 (1989) 283–300.
Lunn, Nicholas P. *The Original Ending of Mark: A New Case for the Authenticity of Mark 16:9–20.* Eugene, OR: Pickwick, 2014.
Magness, J. Lee. *Sense and Absence: Structure and Suspension in the Ending of Mark's Gospel.* Atlanta: Scholars Press, 1986.
Malbon, Elizabeth Struthers. "Fallible Followers: Women and Men in the Gospel of Mark." *Semeia* 28 (1983) 29–48.
———. *In the Company of Jesus: Characters in Mark's Gospel.* Louisville: Westminster John Knox, 2000.
———. "The Jewish Leaders in the Gospel of Mark." *JBL* 108 (1989) 259–81.

Bibliography

———. "The Major Importance of the Minor Characters in Mark." In *The New Literary Criticism and the New Testament*, edited by Elizabeth Struthers Malbon and Edgar V. McKnight, 58–86. JSNTSup 109. Sheffield: Sheffield Academic, 1994.

———. *Mark's Jesus: Characterization as Narrative Christology*. Waco, TX: Baylor University Press, 2009.

———. "Narrative Criticism: How Does the Story Mean?" In *Mark and Method: New Approaches to Biblical Studies*, 2nd ed., edited by Janice Capel Andersen and Stephen D. Moore, 29–57. Minneapolis: Fortress, 2008.

———. *Narrative Space and Mythic Meaning in Mark*. New Voices in Biblical Studies. San Francisco: Harper & Row, 1986.

———. "The Poor Widow in Mark and Her Poor Rich Readers." *CBQ* 53 (1991) 589–604.

———. "'Reflected Christology': An Aspect of Narrative 'Christology' in the Gospel of Mark." *PRSt* 26 (1999) 127–45.

———. "Text and Contexts: Interpreting the Disciples in Mark." *Semeia* 62 (1993) 81–102.

Marcus, Joel. *Mark*. 2 vols. AB 27–27A. New Haven: Yale University Press, 2000–2009.

Marguerat, Daniel, and Yvan Bourquin. *How to Read Bible Stories: An Introduction to Narrative Criticism*. Translated by John Bowden. London: SCM, 1999.

Marshall, Christopher D. *Faith as a Theme in Mark's Narrative*. SNTSMS 64. Cambridge: Cambridge University Press, 1989.

Meier, John P. *Companions and Competitors*. Vol. 3 of *A Marginal Jew: Rethinking the Historical Jesus*. ABRL. New York: Doubleday, 2001.

Metzger, Bruce M. *A Textual Commentary on the Greek New Testament: A Companion Volume to the United Bible Societies' Greek New Testament (Fourth rev. ed.)*. 2nd ed. Stuttgart: Deutsche Bibelgesellschaft, 1994.

Miller, Susan. "Women Characters in Mark's Gospel." In *Character Studies and the Gospel of Mark*, edited by Christopher W. Skinner and Matthew Ryan Hauge, 174–93. LNTS 483. London: T. & T. Clark, 2014.

———. *Women in Mark's Gospel*. JSNTSup 259. London: T. & T. Clark, 2004.

Mitchell, Joan L. *Beyond Fear and Silence: A Feminist-Literary Reading of Mark*. London: Continuum, 2001.

Moloney, Francis J. *The Gospel of Mark*. Grand Rapids: Baker Academic, 2002.

———. "The Vocation of the Disciples in the Gospel of Mark." In *A Hard Saying: The Gospel and Culture*, 53–84. Collegeville, MN: Liturgical, 2001.

Morrison, Gregg S. *The Turning Point in the Gospel of Mark: A Study in Markan Christology*. Eugene, OR: Pickwick, 2014.

Moss, Candida. "The Man with the Flow of Power: Porous Bodies in Mark 5:25–34." *JBL* 129 (2010) 507–19.

Munro, Winsome. "Women Disciples in Mark?" *CBQ* 44 (1982) 225–41.

Naluparayil, Jacob Chacko. *The Identity of Jesus in Mark: An Essay on Narrative Christology*. SBFA 49. Jerusalem: Franciscan Printing Press, 2000.

Nanos, Mark D. "Paul's Reversal of Jews Calling Gentiles 'Dogs' (Philippians 3:2): 1600 Years of an Ideological Tale Wagging an Exegetical Dog? *BibInt* 17 (2009) 448–82.

Neville, David J. "Creation Reclaimed: Resurrection and Responsibility in Mark 15:40—16:8." In *Resurrection and Responsibility: Essays on Theology, Scripture, and Ethics in Honour of Thorwald Lorenzen*, edited by Keith D. Dyer and David J. Neville, 95–115. Eugene, OR: Pickwick, 2009.

Bibliography

———. *A Peaceable Hope: Contesting Violent Eschatology in the New Testament Narratives*. Studies in Peace and Scripture 11. Grand Rapids: Baker Academic, 2013.
———. *The Vehement Jesus: Grappling with Troubling Gospel Texts*. Studies in Peace and Scripture 15. Eugene, OR: Cascade, 2017.
Nineham, Dennis E. *The Gospel of St Mark*. Penguin New Testament Commentaries. Baltimore: Penguin, 1963.
Noh, Eun-Ju. *Metarepresentation: A Relevance-Theory Approach*. Amsterdam: John Benjamins, 2000.
Pennington, Jonathan T. *Reading the Gospels Wisely: A Narrative and Theological Introduction*. Grand Rapids: Baker Academic, 2012.
———. *The Sermon on the Mount and Human Flourishing: A Theological Commentary*. Grand Rapids: Baker Academic, 2017.
Peterson, Norman R. "When Is the End Not the End? Literary Reflections on the Ending of Mark's Narrative." *Int* 34 (1980) 151–66.
Powell, Mark Alan. "Narrative Criticism." In *Hearing the New Testament: Strategies for Interpretation*, edited by Joel B. Green, 239–55. Grand Rapids: Eerdmans, 1995.
———. "Narrative Criticism: The Emergence of a Prominent Reading Strategy." In *Mark as Story: Retrospect and Prospect*, edited by Kelly R. Iverson and Christopher W. Skinner, 19–43. RBS 65. Atlanta: Society of Biblical Literature, 2011.
———. "Toward a Narrative-Critical Understanding of Mark." *Int* 47 (1993) 341–46.
———. *What Is Narrative Criticism?* GBS. Minneapolis: Fortress, 1990.
Resseguie, James L. *Narrative Criticism of the New Testament: An Introduction*. Grand Rapids: Baker Academic, 2005.
Rhoads, David. "Jesus and the Syrophoenician Woman in Mark: A Narrative-Critical Study." *JAAR* 62 (1994) 343–75.
———. "Narrative Criticism and the Gospel of Mark." *JAAR* 50 (1982) 411–26.
Rhoads, David, and Donald Michie. *Mark as Story: An Introduction to the Narrative of a Gospel*. Philadelphia: Fortress, 1982.
Rhoads, David, Joanna Dewey, and Donald Michie. *Mark as Story: An Introduction to the Narrative of a Gospel*. 2nd ed. Minneapolis: Fortress, 1999.
———. *Mark as Story: An Introduction to the Narrative of a Gospel*. 3rd ed. Minneapolis: Fortress, 2012.
Sabin, Marie Noonan. *Reopening the Word: Reading Mark as Theology in the Context of Early Judaism*. Oxford: Oxford University Press, 2002.
Schnabel, Eckhard J. *Mark*. TNTC 2. Downers Grove, IL: InterVarsity, 2017.
Schottroff, Luise. *Let the Oppressed Go Free: Feminist Perspectives on the New Testament*. Translated by Annemarie S. Kidder. Gender and the Biblical Tradition. Louisville: Westminster John Knox, 1993.
Schüssler Fiorenza, Elisabeth. *In Memory of Her: A Feminist Theological Reconstruction of Christian Origins*. New York: Crossroad, 1983.
Selvidge, Marla J. "Mark 5:25–34 and Leviticus 15:19–20: A Reaction to Restrictive Purity Regulations." *JBL* 103 (1984) 619–23.
Senior, Donald. *The Passion of Jesus in the Gospel of Mark*. Delaware: Glazier, 1984.
Shepherd, Tom. "The Narrative Function of Markan Intercalation." *NTS* 41 (1995) 522–40.
Sim, Margaret G. *Marking Thought and Talk in New Testament Greek: New Light from Linguistics on the Particles ἵνα and ὅτι*. Cambridge: James Clarke & Co., 2010.
Skinner, Christopher W. "The Study of Character(s) in the Gospel of Mark: A Survey of Research from Wrede to the Performance Critics (1901 to 2014)." In *Character*

Bibliography

Studies in the Gospel of Mark, edited by Christopher W. Skinner and Matthew Ryan Hauge, 3-34. LNTS 483. London: T. & T. Clark, 2014.
Smith, Stephen H. *A Lion with Wings: A Narrative-Critical Approach to Mark's Gospel.* Sheffield: Sheffield Academic, 1996.
Stein, Robert H. "The Ending of Mark." *BBR* 18 (2008) 79-98.
―――. *Jesus, the Temple, and the Coming of the Son of Man: A Commentary on Mark 13.* Downers Grove, IL: InterVarsity, 2014.
―――. *Mark.* BECNT. Grand Rapids: Baker Academic, 2008.
Sternberg, Meir. *The Poetics of Biblical Narrative: Ideological Literature and the Drama of Reading.* Bloomington: Indiana University Press, 1985.
Strange, James F., and Hershel Shanks. "Has the House Where Jesus Stayed in Capernaum Been Found?" *BAR* 8 (1982) 26-37.
Strauss, Mark L. *Mark.* Zondervan Exegetical Commentary on the New Testament. Grand Rapids: Zondervan, 2014.
Sugirtharajah, R. S. "The Widow's Mites Revalued." *ExpTim* 103 (1991) 42-43.
Swartley, Willard M. "The Role of Women in Mark's Gospel: A Narrative Analysis." *BTB* 27 (1997) 16-22.
Tannehill, Robert C. "Disciples in Mark: The Function of a Narrative Role." *JR* 57 (1977) 386-405.
―――. "The Gospel of Mark as Narrative Christology." *Semeia* 16 (1979) 57-95.
Telford, William R. *The Theology of the Gospel of Mark.* New Testament Theology. Cambridge: Cambridge University Press, 1999.
Tetlow, Elizabeth M. *Women and Ministry in the New Testament.* New York: Paulist, 1980.
Theissen, Gerd. *The Gospels in Context: Social and Political History in the Synoptic Tradition.* Translated by Linda M. Maloney. Minneapolis: Fortress, 1991.
―――. *The Miracle Stories of the Early Christian Tradition.* Translated by Francis McDonagh. SNTW. Edinburgh: T. & T. Clark, 1983.
Tolbert, Mary Ann. *Sowing the Gospel: Mark's World in Literary-Historical Perspective.* Minneapolis: Fortress, 1989.
Tyson, Joseph B. "The Blindness of the Disciples in Mark." *JBL* 80 (1961) 261-68.
Vanhoozer, Kevin J. *Faith Speaking Understanding: Performing the Drama of Doctrine.* Louisville: Westminster John Knox, 2014.
―――. *Pictures at a Theological Exhibition: Scenes of the Church's Worship, Witness and Wisdom.* Downers Grove, IL: InterVarsity, 2016.
Wegener, Mark I. *Cruciformed: The Literary Impact of Mark's Story of Jesus and His Disciples.* Lanham, MD: University Press of America, 1995.
Williams, Guy J. "Narrative Space, Angelic Revelation, and the End of Mark's Gospel." *JSNT* 35 (2013) 263-84.
Williams, Joel F. "Literary Approaches to the End of Mark's Gospel." *JETS* 42 (1999) 21-35.
―――. "Mark 7:27: Jesus' Puzzling Statement." In *Interpreting the New Testament: Introduction to the Art and Science of Exegesis*, edited by Darrell L. Bock and Buist M. Fanning, 341-50. Wheaton: Crossway, 2006.
―――. *Other Followers of Jesus: Minor Characters as Major Figures in Mark's Gospel.* JSNTSup 102. Sheffield: JSOT, 1994.
Witherington III, Ben. *Women in the Ministry of Jesus: A Study of Jesus' Attitudes to Women and Their Roles as Reflected in His Earthly Life.* SNTSMS. Cambridge: Cambridge University Press, 1984.

Bibliography

Wright, Addison. "The Widow's Mites: Praise or Lament?—A Matter of Context" *CBQ* 44 (1982) 256–65.

Index of Authors

Aernie, Jeffrey W., 40
Alonso, Pablo, 78
Aquino, Frederick D., 75, 106
Aune, David E., 62

Barton, Stephen C., 92, 95-96, 98
Bates, Matthew W., 5
Bauckham, Richard, 40, 54-55, 63, 97, 104, 107-8, 110-11
Bayer, Hans F., 42, 57-58, 93, 95, 109
Beavis, Mary Ann, 37, 53, 63, 90, 92
Bengston, Hermann, 70
Bennema, Cornelis, 13, 19-24, 26-27, 34
Best, Ernest, 36
Betsworth, Sharon, 38, 60, 65, 81
Black, C. Clifton, 29, 50, 53, 95
Bolt, Peter, 84
Boring, M. Eugene, 36, 38, 50, 53, 65, 73, 84, 89, 93, 111
Bourquin, Yvan, 10
Broadhead, Edwin, 36, 95, 99
Burer, Michael H., 19
Burnett, Fred W., 20

Cadwallader, Alan H., 73, 79
Calvin, John, 97
Camery-Hoggatt, Jerry, 75
Catchpole, David, 108
Charry, Ellen T., 5
Chatman, Seymour, 16
Clarke, Andrew D., 55
Cohen, Shaye, 58-59
Collins, Adela Yarbo, 17, 54, 56, 62-63, 78, 80, 84, 88, 93-94, 102, 111-12

Cotes, Mary, 106

D'Angelo, Mary Rose, 59-60, 106
Danove, Paul L., 30, 36, 106, 110-11
Davidsen, Ole, 36
Dewey, Joanna, 9, 12, 15, 17, 19, 23, 58, 106
Dibelius, Martin, 85
DiCicco, Mario, 86, 91
Donahue, John R., 50, 53, 61, 70, 72, 80, 85, 88, 95, 98
Driggers, Ira Brent, 14, 102
Dwyer, Timothy, 63, 108, 111

Edwards, James R., 37, 53, 73, 77-78, 80, 84, 95
Ernst, Josef, 53
Evans, Craig A., 85, 98, 109
Ewen, Yosef, 20

Fander, Monika, 37
Fonrobert, Charlotte, 59
Forster, E.M., 19-20, 24
Fowler, Robert M., 106
France, R.T., 52-53, 58, 69, 78, 84, 89-91, 93, 104-6

Garland, David E., 30, 35, 42
Getty-Sullivan, Mary Ann, 98
Gorman, Michael J., 33, 115-17
Grassi, Joseph A., 95
Guelich, Robert A., 58, 64, 74, 80
Gundry, Robert, 53-54, 85, 109

Haber, Susan, 57, 59-61, 65

Index of Authors

Harrington, Daniel J., 50, 53, 61, 70, 72, 80, 85, 88, 95, 98
Hays, Richard B., 3, 33
Henderson, Suzanne Watts, 30, 36
Hester, David, 106
Hooker, Morna D., 38, 64, 84, 89, 92, 94–95, 98
Hurtado, Larry W., 30, 33, 34, 36, 40, 62, 84, 94–95, 99, 102, 106–9, 112–14

Iverson, Kelly R., 9, 21, 72–74, 78

Juel, Donald, 106

Kähler, Martin, 101
Kelhoffer, James A., 95, 103
Kingsbury, Jack Dean, 36
Kinukawa, Hisako, 37, 105
Krause, Deborah, 54

Lane, William L., 53
Lincoln, Andrew T., 38, 106–7, 111
Lunn, Nicholas P., 14, 102

Magness, J. Lee, 107
Malbon, Elizabeth Struthers, 10, 16, 19–21, 24–25, 33–38, 40, 51–52, 54, 63, 70–71, 80, 88, 91–92, 95, 97, 103–4, 108, 112–14
Marcus, Joel, 49, 53–54, 58–59, 63, 70–71, 74, 84–85, 87, 90, 93–95, 99, 111
Marguerat, Daniel, 10
Marshall, Christopher D., 58, 62–64, 71
McLemore, A. Brian, 75, 106
Meier, John P., 37
Metzger, Bruce M., 14, 102
Michie, Donald, 9, 12, 15, 17, 19, 23
Miller, Susan, 2, 37–38, 49–50, 53, 55, 57–58, 65, 71, 72, 75, 78–79, 81, 90–91, 95–96, 98, 104, 112, 115
Mitchell, Joan L., 37, 106
Moloney, Francis J., 14, 30, 38, 54, 60–61, 64, 71, 84, 90, 92, 94–95, 98, 104, 111
Morrison, Gregg S., 36
Moss, Candida, 56–57

Munro, Winsome, 37, 105

Naluparayil, Jacob Chacko, 36
Nanos, Mark D., 72
Neville, David J., 3, 83, 109–10
Nineham, Dennis E., 85, 94
Noh, Eun-Ju, 76

Pennington, Jonathan T., 5, 17, 26
Peterson, Norman R., 106
Powell, Mark Alan, 10–14, 16–17, 22

Resseguie, James L., 10–11, 19
Rhoads, David, 9–10, 12, 15, 17, 19, 23, 75, 80

Sabin, Marie Noonan, 97
Schnabel, Eckhard J., 53, 70
Schottroff, Luise, 53, 55
Schüssler Fiorenza, Elisabeth, 33, 61, 97–98, 104
Selvidge, Marla J., 58
Senior, Donald, 95
Shanks, Hershel, 49
Shepherd, Tom, 55, 95
Sim, Margaret G., 77
Skinner, Christopher W., 9, 29
Smith, Stephen H., 25
Stein, Robert H., 14, 30, 53, 59, 63, 73, 84, 90, 92, 94–95, 98, 102
Sternberg, Meir, 12
Strange, James F., 49
Strauss, Mark L., 32, 64, 95
Sugirtharajah, R.S., 85, 87
Swartley, Willard M., 37

Tannehill, Robert C., 2, 30, 32–33, 36, 40–41
Telford, William R., 2
Tetlow, Elizabeth M., 37
Theissen, Gerd, 53, 69–70, 80
Tolbert, Mary Ann, 63, 104, 106
Tyson, Joseph B., 106

Vanhoozer, Kevin J., 96, 123

Wegener, Mark I., 15
Williams, Guy J., 111

Index of Authors

Williams, Joel F., 14, 24–25, 37, 42, 51, 63, 76–78, 90–92, 95, 97, 102, 104, 110

Witherington III, Ben, 53, 70, 105

Wright, Addison, 85–87, 89

Index of Ancient Sources

OLD TESTAMENT

Exodus

22:31 — 73

Leviticus

12:7 — 58
15:19–33 — 58
20:18 — 58

Deuteronomy

15:11 — 94

Judges

6:22–23 — 31, 111

1 Samuel

17:43 — 73

1 Kings

21:23 — 73
22:38 — 73

2 Kings

8:13 — 73
9:6 — 73

Psalms

37 — 104
37:12 — 104

Proverbs

26:11 — 73

Isaiah

1:17 — 84
1:23 — 84
6:9–13 — 77
6:9–10 — 77
6:13 — 77
56:10–11 — 73

Jeremiah

7:6 — 84

Ezekiel

22:7 — 84

Daniel

8:17 — 31, 111
10:7 — 31, 111
10:12 — 31, 111

Zechariah

7:10 — 84

NEW TESTAMENT

Matthew

7:6 — 73
13:15 — 77
15:21–28 — 39

Index of Ancient Sources

Matthew *(continued)*

20:2	92
26:8–9	39

Mark

1–14	38
1	47, 54, 85, 103, 109
1:1—16:8	14
1:1—8:21	32
1:1	11, 79
1:13	53
1:14–15	4, 41, 67
1:16–20	29–30, 42
1:21–28	50–51
1:22	88
1:27	93
1:29–34	47
1:29–31	2, 5–6, 20, 23, 26, 39, 42, 47–48, 54, 65, 67, 69, 71, 80, 85, 113, 116, 120
1:29	116
1:30	50
1:31	50, 52, 54
1:32–34	51
1:38	67
1:40–45	47
1:40–44	60
1:44	108–9
2:1–12	47
2:1–5	71
2:1	68
2:2	78
2:6	88
2:9	50
2:11	50
2:12	53
2:13–17	60
2:13–14	30
2:16	88
2:18–28	30
2:18–22	94
3:1–5	32, 47
3:3	50
3:7–12	74
3:10	62
3:13–19	30
3:14	42, 67
3:19	31
3:20–35	2, 30
3:20	68
3:22	88
3:27	73
3:31–35	38, 65
3:34	31
4	31, 63, 77, 111
4:9	78
4:11–12	77
4:11	77
4:12	32, 77
4:13	77
4:23	78
4:26–32	77
4:28	73
4:33	78
4:35–41	31
4:37–41	63, 111
4:41	63, 111
5	47, 60, 71
5:1–20	59, 64, 74
5:15	64, 111
5:21–43	47
5:21–24	2, 37, 48, 50, 64, 69, 72
5:22–23	72
5:24–29	71
5:24	62
5:25–34	2–3, 5–6, 26, 37, 39, 42, 47–48, 55, 65, 67, 69, 71, 80, 111, 113, 120
5:25–26	56–57
5:27	62, 71
5:29	57
5:31	62
5:33	63, 71
5:34	61, 63–64, 87
5:35–43	2, 37, 48, 50, 57, 64, 69, 72
5:35–36	71
5:35	78
5:36	78, 111
5:41	50, 79
5:42–43	53
5:42	60
6–8	74
6	31, 74
6:3	38, 102
6:12–13	30

Index of Ancient Sources

6:14–29	2, 38, 102, 112	9:14–29	47, 50
6:20	111	9:14–27	71
6:30–44	32, 74, 80	9:27	50
6:30	30	9:30–37	35, 115
6:42	74	9:31	32
6:45–52	31	9:32	32, 111
6:49	31	9:35–37	33, 42, 88
6:50	111	9:35	81
6:52	31, 80	10:17–31	52, 90
6:56	62	10:21	90, 93
7	67, 74, 76	10:26	93
7:1–23	30, 60, 75–77, 81	10:31	91
7:1–5	74, 88	10:32–45	35, 88, 115–16
7:6–13	75	10:32–34	32
7:14–15	75	10:32	111
7:17–23	75–76	10:33	89
7:18–23	75, 77	10:35–41	32
7:18	77, 80	10:42–45	33, 42, 105
7:24–36	47	10:45	23, 53, 86, 88–89, 116
7:24–30	2, 5–6, 14, 26, 37, 39, 42, 48, 62, 68, 81, 113, 120	10:46–52	37, 47, 51, 54
7:25–26	72	10:49	50
7:25	71	10:52	71
7:26	70	11–15	86
7:27	68, 72, 74–75, 79	11–13	84, 91
7:28	74	11–12	83, 92
7:29–30	78	11	83
7:31—8:10	74	11:1–11	83
7:31–37	32	11:11	83
7:36	109	11:15–19	83
8	74, 86	11:18	88, 111
8:1–10	32, 80	11:27—12:40	83
8:1–9	74	11:27–28	79, 88
8:8	74	11:29	78–79
8:14–21	32, 80	11:31–33	79
8:17–18	32	11:31	93
8:22—10:52	32	11:32	111
8:22–26	32, 47, 54	12	82, 85, 88, 90, 97
8:31–38	35, 88, 115	12:7	93
8:31	32, 89	12:12	111
8:32–33	32	12:18–27	2
8:34–38	32, 34, 82, 91, 105	12:28–34	90
8:34–35	81	12:30	90
8:34	96, 100, 115	12:33	90
8:35	86	12:34	91
8:38	33, 78	12:35–40	88
9:6	111	12:38–44	95
9:11–12	73	12:38–40	84–85
		12:40	84

Index of Ancient Sources

Mark (continued)

12:41–44	2, 5–6, 14, 20, 26, 37, 39, 42, 83–84, 86, 91, 97, 100, 113, 120
12:41	87–88
12:42	87–89
12:43	88
12:44	88–89, 95
13–16	33
13	33, 84, 92, 97
13:1–2	84–85
13:1	83
13:5–8	33
13:5	42
13:9–11	33
13:10	73
13:31	78
14–15	83, 86, 92, 97
14	31, 33, 82, 92, 96
14:1–2	95
14:1	88, 93
14:3–9	2–3, 5–6, 26, 37, 39, 42, 54, 83, 91, 96, 100, 113, 120
14:3	92–93, 97
14:4	39, 93
14:5	92–93
14:6	94
14:7	94
14:8	94–95, 98
14:9	97–99
14:10–11	95–96
14:17–20	33
14:27	33
14:28	50, 110
14:30	33
14:43–45	33, 96
14:43	89
14:50–52	33, 96, 103, 105
14:50	110
14:51–52	111
14:52	110
14:53	89
14:54	104, 109
14:66–72	2, 29, 33, 38–39, 96, 103–5
15–16	26, 38–40, 42, 96–97, 101–3, 107–8, 112–14, 117
15	54, 102, 105
15:1	89
15:21	51
15:31	89
15:39	51
15:40–41	2, 5–6, 23, 26, 39, 54, 96, 102–5, 116–17, 120
15:40	109, 112
15:41	2, 5–6, 53–54, 116
15:47	2, 26, 39, 54, 96, 102, 104–5, 117, 120
16	103, 105, 109
16:1–8	2, 5–6, 27, 39, 54, 96, 108, 117, 20
16:1–7	105
16:1	54, 97, 102, 104
16:3	93
16:5–8	64
16:5	111–12
16:6–8	38
16:6–7	99
16:6	49–51, 102, 113, 116
16:7–8	39
16:7	29, 34, 106, 109, 113
16:8	96, 102, 105–12, 114
16:9–20	14, 102

Luke

2:9–10	31, 111
24:11–12	39

John

12:4–5	39

Romans

1:16	70, 73

1 Corinthians

1:22–24	70
1:23	116

Philippians

3:2	73

2 Peter

2:22	73

Index of Ancient Sources

Revelation
1:17 — 31, 111
22:15 — 73

DEAD SEA SCROLLS
11QTemple^a
45:7–17 — 58
46:16–18 — 58
48:14–17 — 58

RABBINC WRITINGS
Leviticus Rabbah
3.5 — 86

Midrash Psalms
22.31 — 86

Mishnah Niddah
7:4 — 58

GRECO-ROMAN WRITINGS
Josephus
Against Apion
1.71 — 70

Antiquities
3.261 — 58
14.313–321 — 70

Jewish War
2.478 — 70

Xenophon
Memorabilia
1.3.3 — 86

NEW TESTAMENT APOCRYPHA AND PSEUDEPIGRAPHA
Pseudo-Clementines
Homilies
13.7 — 70

www.ingramcontent.com/pod-product-compliance
Lightning Source LLC
Chambersburg PA
CBHW051943160426
43198CB00013B/2277